D0525145

THE FAT LADIES CLUB

The Fat Ladies Club

The Tale of Five Friends Facing the
Fearful Prospect of
First-Time Pregnancy

* * *

HILARY GARDENER, ANDREA BETTRIDGE,
SARAH GROVES, ANNETTE JONES
AND LYNDSEY LAWRENCE

PENGUIN BOOKS

PENGUIN BOOKS

Published by the Penguin Group
Penguin Books Ltd, 80 Strand, London WC2R 0RL, England
Penguin Putnam Inc., 375 Hudson Street, New York, New York 10014, USA
Penguin Books Australia Ltd, 250 Camberwell Road, Camberwell, Victoria 3124, Australia
Penguin Books Canada Ltd, 10 Alcorn Avenue, Toronto, Ontario, Canada M4V 3B2
Penguin Books India (P) Ltd, 11, Community Centre, Panchsheel Park, New Delhi – 110 017, India
Penguin Books (NZ) Ltd, Cnr Rosedale and Airborne Roads, Albany, Auckland, New Zealand
Penguin Books (South Africa) (Pty) Ltd, 24 Sturdee Avenue, Rosebank 2196, South Africa

Penguin Books Ltd, Registered Offices: 80 Strand, London WC2R 0RL, England

www.penguin.com

First published by author.co.uk 1999
Published by Fat Ladies Publishing 2000
Published in Penguin Books 2002

6

Set in 11/13 pt Monotype Bembo
Typeset by Rowland Phototypesetting Ltd, Bury St Edmunds, Suffolk
Printed in England by Clays Ltd, St Ives plc

Dedication

This book is dedicated to all of our children, but especially to Emily and Megan, the daughters of our dear friend and fellow author, Annette.

Hilary, Andrea, Sarah and Lyndsey

Contents

Acknowledgements

A special thank-you goes to Mary Green, who donated the wonderful illustrations, which so magically bring to life the text.

Also, to our husbands, David, Bruce, Tim, Gavin and Tim, for tolerating their newly imposed extended family in the form of us, the Fat Ladies Club.

The Founder Members of the Fat Ladies Club

Hilary Gardener – *Gobby Girlie*. Hilary is our farmer's wife, who has been known to lamb a couple of ewes before heading off to her day job as a learning-disabilities nurse. She is renowned for being a total motor-mouth with a wicked wit, which frequently gets her into trouble.

Sarah Groves – *Gorgeous Girlie*. Sarah is our multilingual international jet-setter who divides her time between Spain and England. Sarah has an amazing ability always to look immaculate and exude warmth from her smile, no matter what time of day you catch her.

Lyndsey Lawrence – *Genius Girlie*. Lyndsey is our mad scientist! We love to imagine her in work wearing a lab coat, surrounded by flaming Bunsen burners and bubbling test tubes. Not only does she have to endure this constant ribbing from us, but she is also the long-suffering wife of a rugby-obsessed Welshman.

Andrea Bettridge – *Goalie Girlie*. Andrea is our Greek policewoman who is fanatical about Arsenal FC. She is a complete tomboy, who is proud to say that she has never owned a lipstick in her life. She's a keen footballer for the local ladies' team and has become well known for her spectacular, diving-goalie saves.

Annette Jones – *Genuine Girlie*. Annette is our quiet and caring voice of reason. She is a suit-clad, city-slicking accountant by day, and as soft as butter by night. Really she is the dark horse of our club, though. Take her wedding day, for example . . .

READ ON!!

Meet the Girlies

If you are reading this and it is in a book with more than two pages, then a miracle has occurred! We have been successful in our venture – to give you a taste of all the emotional upheavals and physical changes, humorous and horrendous, which we have experienced throughout our pregnancies and the early months of motherhood.

So much happens in such a short space of time. If you had told any one of the five of us just one year ago where we'd be now, we would have laughed in your face. Me, a mother, with a real baby, doing coffee mornings with other mums, pushing prams, changing nappies and doing baby talk? Absolutely no way!

We had all hit our late twenties and early thirties and felt that the old biological clocks were ticking, and that it was a case of now or never, before the perks of a double income and being fancy free became necessities we could not give up. So – *now* it was!

We met through the local NHS antenatal classes, and we have learnt so much about each other over the months – we are all astounded that five such diverse characters have come out of this experience knowing so many intimate details about each other and being such good friends. We have lived through each other's traumas and triumphs so closely that we thought you could also gain from our open and honest detailed discussions.

Other books will give you the factual stuff – what physical changes you can expect, the development of the foetus, etc. Well, forget the textbook theory now and settle down for what amounts to an eavesdrop into our girlie chats. There will be no facts, no figures – just pure unadulterated detail on all the bits you really wanted to know about but were afraid to ask!

Did we get stretch marks – how many, where and what are they really like?
What happened to our sex lives?
Did 'it' feel the same afterwards?
When did we feel like 'mums'?

We've all been very lucky, really, in that we each had relatively straightforward pregnancies and early months, so there will be no detailed horror stories, just entertaining anecdotes which most women, we hope, will be able to relate to.

In order to bring you this alternative guide to the real ins and outs of pregnancy and motherhood, we have endured many a long evening sitting gossiping with a bottle of wine or two, while our husbands have had the pleasure of the company of our little treasures. This has obviously been a harrowing ordeal for us all . . . but we hope the end result is worth it! So sit back, relax. It's now time to . . . meet the girlies.

Hilary

* * *

Who am I? Where do I come from? This is all a bit deep and meaningful for my liking, so I will keep it as brief as is possible for a woman with a severe case of verbal diarrhoea!

Well, I am twenty-nine years old and a community learning-disability nurse by profession. This basically means that I am lucky enough to spend my days out and about visiting adults who live in the community who have a learning disability (or mental handicap as it used to be termed). I absolutely love my job and even now, as I write this while I am on maternity leave, I cannot imagine ever not working in this capacity. I already blackheads, but this was probably due to an inexplicable hatred for cleanliness at the time. I thought that drinking Southern Comfort, smoking menthol cigarettes and constantly talking in quotations (wiggling my fingers in the air to indicate speech marks) made me one of the hippest chicks in town. Not to mention, of course, my obsession with Bertolt Brecht the playwright. I bored David and many others senseless with my constant references to him. David fortunately had known me before I began this bizarre phase and stuck by me through it, although I must say that I have paid my penance for it over the past twelve years, as he still finds it a source of great amusement to make me the butt of many a joke by recounting stories from this era.

Once I had recovered from this grim phase, I then went off to do my learning-disability-nurse training, and to pickle my liver at the hospital social club next to the nurses' accommodation where I lived. David went to agricultural college at this time, and learnt more agriculturally themed lyrics to rugby songs than he ever learnt about the farming industry itself.

Our qualifications, reputations and relationship somehow survived these three years, and we then decided to take a year out to go travelling – separately. David set off with a couple of buddies from college to discover just how many different beers there are between England and Australia, while I went with a lifelong friend and a whole different agenda. We managed to see and do things that I now find difficult to believe myself. We watched open-heart surgery in India, we got arrested in Goa, we did bar work in Hong Kong and hippy-style hair wraps for other backpackers in Australia, New Zealand and America in order to make enough money to get to the next place each day. I could write pages and pages about backpacking – it was definitely the best year of my life. As the saying goes, once you have got the travelling bug, it is the hardest disease to cure. I have been back from travelling now for nearly six years and I can honestly say that barely a day goes by without the thought going through my mind of getting on a plane with just a backpack and no plans. At the time I absolutely loved sleeping in dormitories, I loved only having half a dozen items of clothing to chose from and I loved not knowing where I would be the next night. But when I think now about my intolerance of snoring, my extensive wardrobe and my obsessive need for order in my life, I cannot actually imagine how I coped!

Now for a quick analysis of my personality. I am quite an outgoing person, who can definitely talk for England. David's favourite expression, after a night out with company, is 'Put your mouth in neutral now, love – it's time we went home and gave these poor people's ears a rest.' Having said that, I am sure that half the reason I talk so much is because I am quite a nervous person inside. It is a bit like that age-old cure for travel sickness – keep eating, you cannot bring up food while you are still pushing it down. I do the same with words – keep talking, you cannot get nervous while you are too busy concentrating on the absolute twaddle you are churning out! I think that taking theatre studies A-level helped in this area as well – I do not remember ever opening my mouth in public before that.

Since David and I came back from travelling we have basically just worked, played hockey and had holidays. It is amazing how quickly the time has gone and how easily we became comfortable with just the two of us and a healthy joint income. We live by the farming calendar, with the most important dates being tup-ping (that is when the boys meet the girls in the sheep world), lambing, shearing and harvest (when David helps his brother who is an arable farmer). I help with lambing each year and have become quite a dab hand at doing the James Herriot bit with my arm up the back end of a ewe. I have to take annual leave from my job at this time each year so that I can do some of the night shifts in order to give David a break. Holidays have to fit in with these farming milestones and with the hockey season. David plays at first-team level and will not miss a game if he can help it. I also play hockey, but at a very social level, preferably never leaving the club's well-stocked bar! I took up the sport more from fear of being a hockey widow than from a deep desire to take up the sport, but as a result our weekend social life does now revolve around our circle of hockey friends.

Children. How do they fit in? Boy, now that is a good question? Having had a car accident when I was nineteen which left a big question mark over my ability to conceive, I had lived my life trying to convince myself that children were not going to fit into our busy lifestyle. When I hit twenty-eight, I decided that it was a case of now or never, because if I was going to need any medical help, I could not afford to put off trying any longer. 'Trying for children' is such a funny expression. I certainly did not feel grown-up enough to try consciously, and we were not mentally prepared to give up or adapt our lives yet. So we casually decided to leave things to Fate for a while and see what happened.

Fate happened pretty quickly, and I have never had such horrendously mixed emotions in all my life! I was so thrilled that I could get pregnant, having lived for nearly ten years not knowing, but I was also unbelievably petrified that I was actually pregnant. I almost grieved for my familiar life. All I could see ahead were no more Saturday nights out having a bevvy, no more expensive holidays abroad, no more lie-ins (I love my sleep), and it all felt as though it was happening to me and me alone. I remember thinking, 'It's all right for David – he will still be able to play hockey and go out. I will be the one left at home with the blob' (as I had affectionately termed my unborn child). I had images going through my mind of me ringing the hockey club, asking for David and then hearing the whispers as the answer came back that he had just left, even though he would, of course, be standing there with a full pint. My imagination and emotions ran wild!

Everyone I knew who had children seemed to think that they were worth all the sacrifices. However, never really having had any interest in children or babies beyond my one-hour boredom threshold, I could not begin to imagine that an emotion existed strong enough to create a sudden increase in a person's boredom threshold to twenty-four hours a day, seven days a week – let alone that this emotion could ever possibly 'kick in' with me.

Being professionally 'in the know' about all the various things that can go wrong throughout pregnancy and childbirth was a minus, too – things which could potentially leave the child with a learning disability. Much as I love my job, the fearful prospect of having a brain-damaged child was not at all lessened by the fact that I was qualified to provide it with the best care. If anything, the fear was increased. It did not help, therefore, that I discovered I was pregnant the day after I returned from a very boozy weekend in Paris. As if that wasn't enough, I had the beginnings of a throat infection when I went out to Paris and, not wanting to ruin a great weekend, I had used that extremely dubious medical cure of necking vast quantities of Aspirin and red wine all weekend in order to ensure that the infection did not take hold. I had done a pregnancy test before I went to make sure that it was safe for me to use this remedy, but it had been negative then, and only showed up lovely and blue after the potential damage had been done. Fortunately no harm came of it, but unfortunately I had to live through the full pregnancy before believing this possible.

Well, after having all these mixed emotions at discovering I was pregnant, I then started to bleed at six weeks. This felt as though someone had stuck a dirty great pin into a balloon that I had not even realized I'd blown up. I did very little for a few days and the bleeding stopped, but I then had to wait for two more weeks before they would do the scan to check that it was still in there. These were the strangest two weeks ever – am I pregnant or aren't I? I had a recurring nightmare during this time that I would get to the scan and they would say, 'we are sorry, Mrs Gardener, but you have never actually been pregnant. It must have been a bad case of wind.' So when we saw the scan with the little broad bean with a heartbeat in it showing up so clearly on the screen, there was a huge sense of relief that it had not just been my imagination or a faulty pregnancy test. It was

something to do with my propensity to be quite dippy on occasions and my professional misuse of sayings and proverbs. Outbursts such as 'you've got the nail in the nutshell' and 'I feel a lot better with a bit of meat inside me' have earned me the reputation of being either a social embarrassment or a bit of light relief, depending on the company!

I have a very artistic temperament, which leads me to indulge in hobbies such as interior design, inexhaustible DIY projects and dressmaking. My mum still laughs at the time I made myself an outfit out of an old sheet without so much as a pattern. I lay on the fabric getting my mother to draw around me, cut it out, sewed it together and added the finishing touch by tie-dyeing it – very fetching at the time, so I thought. My poor mother deserves a medal for continuing to accompany me along the local high street during my teenage years, with me either dressed in one of my new handmade creations, or with my hair cropped very short. I was infamous during my teens for my self-inflicted short back and sides with a generous amount of scalp showing – my attempt at following punk fashion. Now, having reached the tender age of twenty-nine, I sensibly go to the hairdresser's to have my hair cut, but still enjoy mucking around with material, although admittedly a little more conservatively now! After my English, French and History A-levels (which I came pretty close to flunking) I went on to college to study European business studies. This was a four-year degree course and, if I'm honest, the year abroad was the biggest selling point – the thought of living in France for a whole year was highly attractive. My entire college experience was character-building, but the year abroad, without doubt, added the most to my life's rich tapestry. The fun we had, first of all 'studying' at the partner college (and, yes, 'studying' is in inverted commas for a reason) and then doing work experience, knew no bounds. Let's just say that we lived life to the full.

Isn't it always the way though – just when you're living the life of Reilly, you meet the man of your dreams? A mutual friend had invited me to her twenty-first birthday party in England. I deliberated for a while over whether or not to take anyone with me, but eventually decided to play the cool, single, independent woman flying in from France just for the weekend. This was the night that I was to meet my future husband, Tim. In fact, due to somebody else's juggling of the seating plan, we ended up sitting together and got on like a house on fire, with me managing to preserve a certain 'cool chick' aloofness. However, as any self-respecting female reading this will appreciate, I did not want to limit my recreational activities back in France merely to eating cheese, quaffing good wine, and writing home to a boyfriend in England. That would have been cramping my style far too much. As it was, my sole aim at the time was to appreciate fully the Latin-lover prowess of which all males south of the English Channel are so keen to boast. It really was not part of my game plan to begin courting my future husband whilst in the throes of my student life.

Fortunately, Tim was persistent and visited me on several occasions in France, and he quickly acquired a taste for the French way of life. So it was no surprise to our families and friends when, after three years of knowing each other, we positively jumped at the chance of moving out to Paris. I had finished my degree and had worked in London for a year, and Tim had successfully completed his chartered-accountancy exams. We then spent three glorious years in Paris, living ten minutes from Les Champs Elysées, working madly during the week, exploring Paris restaurants and bars by night and at weekends discovering 'la France profonde' (which I have been told to clarify is the 'posh bird' way of saying French countryside), equipped with mountain bikes and a tent. It was an excellent time of fun and antics, the memories of which we will treasure for ever. As a result we are both confirmed Francophiles.

We returned to the UK three years later, due to career changes, and decided that it was a good idea to have a bit of space from each other to decide in exactly which direction we wished to head. Family and friends perceived us to be the perfect couple – good jobs, cosmopolitan lifestyle, fit and healthy, ambitious and energetic. And so did I, but unfortunately 'commitment' was not a word in Tim's vocabulary at the time. He was already travelling a great deal, but based himself at his parents' home, and I was transferred back to London with BT to continue my job in marketing, where I flat-shared in East Finchley. I decided to be cool and play the 'caszh' London girl about town, while Tim sorted his head out, but mentally I had given him a deadline for a proposal by the end of June. Tim, true to his inimitable style, played close to the edge and proposed within a couple of days of the ultimatum expiring. He must have been psychic.

We both desperately missed our Paris existence, and so it was quite appropriate that Tim should propose over breakfast in the Hotel de Crillon on one of our weekend trips back there. If anyone is aware of just how flash the Hotel de Crillon on Place de la Concorde is, don't start getting a complex – we were not staying at the hotel, which is frequented by stars such as Madonna, but had always promised ourselves breakfast there one day. I think Tim thought that the occasion warranted spending fifteen pounds each on what amounted to a glorified slice of toast and a mug of coffee. Either that or he felt it necessary to bribe me with such a sophisticated venue that I would feel coerced into accepting his proposal.

And so we married and moved into a turn-of-the-century house in middle-class suburbia which was convenient for both our jobs. We enjoyed spending time on DIY projects, holidays abroad mountain biking, and socializing as much as we could with friends in London. Little did we realize how 'out in the sticks' people considered us to be, until on one occasion we met up with a family in London who described us to the taxi driver as their 'country bumpkin relatives'. Yes, we were insulted, and made even more effort to get into the city to the theatre and cinema.

It was around April/May that I decided to come off the Pill to let my body's hormones settle back into their natural pattern after seven years of artificial control. 'Huh,' said a midwife friend of mine, 'you'll be hearing the pitter patter of tiny feet before you know it,' but I knew better. Equipped with literature about women's bodies, women's wisdom etc., we embarked on the rhythm method of birth control, which is not, as Hilary thought, 'whipping it out at the crucial moment'. Suddenly I really enjoyed feeling in tune with my body's menstrual cycle and found pleasure in monitoring my fertility by counting the days between periods, and doing the mucus test. Not that I found squidging my mucus intensely enjoyable. It has to be said that testing the contents of your pants to see if the consistency is like egg white, proving that you're very fertile, or thick and sticky, does have its limits. But at least I didn't get as far as taking my temperature every morning. That is obviously for those who practise the rhythm method more seriously. It was all fine until I realized that I was feeling naturally most horny at the time when I was most fertile – which was when I had to abstain. Needless to say, we threw caution to the wind on a couple of occasions and bingo, before we knew it, I was pregnant. With our usual impeccable timing, Tim had just been offered a fantastic new job opportunity, working in Spain all week, every week and returning home at weekends. So right from day one of pregnancy I began to get used to fending for myself.

I first began to wonder if I was pregnant when I met a friend for supper in the local pizza place and out of the blue she said, 'So are you pregnant then?' My instant reply was, 'Of course not – but there again, my period is five days late.' I had supposed that the stresses of a recent conference at work had played havoc with my hormones, but I knew deep down that it would take a hell of a lot more to delay my normal, clockwork-style menstrual cycle. She had got me thinking. *Me* – pregnant? No, it couldn't be possible. We hadn't been purposely trying, so I assumed in some strange way that if the psyche wasn't involved then the body couldn't function independently.

Tim's father had warned him several years prior to us ever meeting that the Groves' sperm was remarkably virulent. We certainly proved him right. Tim and his two brothers had all had the fatherly chat as adolescent boys before their first holidays abroad with their girlfriends. 'Watch out for the hot blood' was the warning, which I assume must have had something to do with male ardour heating up in hot weather! My pregnancy was not wholly planned, but we knew it was safe to put ourselves to the test, considering that we were married and both had good jobs. We just hadn't banked on getting full house straight away.

I didn't suffer the awful morning sickness that a lot of women get, which I was thankful about, especially with Tim not being home during the week. At least by being on my own I was able to indulge in the mini cravings that I felt occasionally – sardines and tomatoes, and tomatoes, and of course, more tomatoes! I cannot boast of any weird and abnormal cravings – I never had the urge to tuck into a jar of pickled gherkins or that legendary lump of coal. I mean, let's face it, how does anyone, least of all a pregnant woman whose brain is shrinking, know that they fancy a lump of coal to chew on? Call me old-fashioned, but I just can't see the attraction. I'll stick with my tomatoes, thanks.

For us, the subject of names became quite an issue early on, particularly because Tim had a shortlist of two names right from the start. He had decided that in order to keep things simple we would reserve the names of our two cats. We have both a male and a female cat, who were, incidentally, both named by Tim. Their names are Gordon and Doris. Much as I like old-fashioned names, I felt I had to draw the line somewhere. I think Jack got off remarkably lightly considering!

The first time I felt properly pregnant was when I felt the first flutter of life in my stomach, when the baby was about eighteen weeks old. I was in Orlando for another work conference and again experiencing the stresses of the job. As I lay in bed trying to get to sleep, practising over and over how I was going to introduce my presentation the following day, I felt the weirdest feeling in my tummy. At first I assumed it was indigestion caused by a pizza I had eaten earlier, but soon realized that it was the famous first flutter. Somehow all the stresses of the next day paled into insignificance. I was going to be a mother!

Lyndsey

* * *

Now to me. Well at thirty-three years of age I am the mummy of the group. No, on second thoughts I'll change that to the big sister of the group. I work as a clinical trials manager testing new drugs on humans for a major pharmaceutical company. I have to say now that my contributions to this book will probably be the shortest of all as I've had endless years of being trained to cut out the waffle and stick to the facts, but here goes!

I was born and bred in the north-east of England and at eighteen I went to University College in Cardiff, where I gained initially a BSc. in Chemistry followed by a Ph.D. in Physical Chemistry. This officially makes me a doctor, but I generally like to keep that quiet as people inevitably ask in which field I work or what the research for my doctorate was about. I sheepishly tell them that my contribution in the scientific field was very consumer orientated. In fact, I studied the effect of the sun, or more specifically the ultra-violet rays, on woollen fabric. The Arabs had a problem with the grey woollen upholstery in their fleets of Mercedes Benz cars, which kept fading in the heat of the

desert sun. So my mission was to amend this problem. However, more pertinent to the average person on the street was the fact that this work also sorted out the problem of how to stop your white woolly jumper going yellow on the washing line. If this has never happened to you then I can say my research was a success!

Anyway, back to the story line. It was while I was working in Cardiff that I met Tim, who is Welsh, and we have now been together for eight years and married for the last four years. We met in a pub one evening when Tim, who was a little worse for wear, made an outstanding first impression with the memorable chat-up line, 'My friend fancies your friend – can we join you?' As you can imagine, my friend and I soon made our excuses and left the pub, only to be pursued by Tim. 'Oh God,' we thought, 'he's a pervert.' So, in an effort to lose him, we went to a neighbour's front door to ensure that he didn't know where we lived. How I had misjudged him – the poor chap actually lived at the far end of our road and wasn't stalking us at all! Anyway, after that romantic start, we subsequently met again five months later, fell in love and have lived happily ever after – so far!

Just before we were married, we both had a bout of wanderlust, and we were lucky enough to live and work in Italy for two years. I was fortunate to find employment in my line of work in Verona, which was our initial passport to Italy. Tim unfortunately could not find employment in his line of work as a business analyst and ended up teaching business English to employees from large companies such as IBM. I do not think that he took his new-found career particularly seriously, but generally used it as an opportunity to teach Italians about that great Welsh passion, rugby, and more importantly the geography of the country itself. He was horrified to discover that they thought Wales was simply a region in England, the same as Tuscany is a region in Italy. He made it his mission to put the record straight, and I believe that to this day there are a number of Italians roaming the streets of Verona with a hint of a Welsh accent and an unhealthy obsession with leeks and red dragons.

Two years later Tim's career was going nowhere, so we reluctantly decided to return to the UK and leave behind the fantastic lifestyle we had come to love so much – the pasta, the wine and of course those zany Italians. I was able to get a transfer with my work, Tim soon found a job, and we started to settle into life back in the UK.

It was no surprise when, eighteen months later, the question of having children became a frequent topic in our conversations. Tim had always been keen, whereas I was not quite as convinced, because I couldn't see how children would fit in with my career, and I seemed to lack the maternal instincts that I thought were the essential requirement to start a family. We kept umming and aahing, and always managed to come up with a reason why it was not the right time. However, when friends who had taken the plunge explained that it could take anything from six months to two years to conceive, the possibility that we might not be able to have children hit home and we decided to throw the towel in and leave it to Fate. Our first attempt at throwing caution to the wind was a complete failure, as halfway through the lovemaking we got cold feet and Tim rushed for the condoms – phew, that was close! It took us another two months before we dared to live dangerously and 'go rubberless'. I remember our initial feelings were of panic, but then we reassured ourselves with our friends' experiences and convinced ourselves that we were fools to think that I would become pregnant so easily. You can imagine our surprise when my next period was late, and it was soon confirmed that I was indeed pregnant. Tim, of course, smugly boasted of his super Welsh sperm, while I contemplated the responsibility that I now had to carry this child for the next forty weeks. No more alcohol, no more soft cheeses and, worse still, no more chocolate mousse!

I have to say our timing wasn't great with regard to our transport arrangements. Having pootled around the streets of Verona in a clapped-out motor, we had always dreamed of having a sports car. When Tim was offered a company car with his new job we decided to take the money and buy the sports car of our dreams. So in the September we carefully chose our Mazda MX5 – the car that was to be Tim's present to me. I couldn't wait for the summer. I was going to be the coolest chick in town, cruising the streets with the roof down, stereo blaring, shades on, blonde hair flowing in the wind – heaven! Oh no, no such luck. We discovered that I was pregnant the week we took delivery of our new car, and by the time the rays of sunshine appeared I was nearly eight months pregnant. This added weight did not entirely fit in with the mental picture I had conjured up – I just about needed a winch to lever me in and out of the car. The hard sports-car suspension became a threat for an early labour as I could feel every bump in the road, so that put paid to my romantic country drives. Mind you, it would have been a handy way to induce labour had I gone overdue. Also it was evident that this car was not going to be the best family car, bearing in mind it only had two seats and a parcel shelf. We may refer to our baby as our little bundle, but realistically she was not going to fit on the shelf behind us! Needless to say, my driving days in our dream car are numbered, and the three of us can never enjoy the car together. We thought that our second car, a five-door hatchback, was going to be perfectly practical until we tried to fit a pram in the boot. I tell you, I don't know how people cope with more than one child – I think you need nothing smaller than a people carrier to accommodate the equipment for just one baby!

Another case of bad timing was Tim's birthday, which was in the month I fell pregnant. Every year we go away with a couple of friends to celebrate each of our birthdays, and Tim's was no exception – we were heading for Barcelona. The evening before we left was the evening that I did the home pregnancy test and found it to be positive. As my period was overdue I had toyed with the idea of waiting to do the test until we came back from Spain. After all, it was only a long weekend, but the thought of not knowing was going to be too much to bear and I did not want to pickle the foetus in the litres of wine that would inevitably be consumed, so the test was done. The next hurdle was keeping the secret from our friends, who, we realized, would become suspicious as soon as the first glass of alcohol was refused, so I decided to feign illness – a tummy upset or something. Since it is not unusual to come a cropper with Spanish tummy, I thought that would be quite convincing, but my plan failed immediately when, at Heathrow, a celebratory birthday drink was called for in duty free. I could hardly complain of Spanish tummy when we had not even left London, so I was already on dodgy ground. I fumbled some excuses at this point, but the truth eventually came out when we were twenty-eight thousand feet above land. Of course, our friends were thrilled, but what a weekend I had watching the three of them consuming copious quantities of wine while I sipped my mineral water. This was going to be a long nine months!

Over all, I had a healthy pregnancy, although it has to be said that I didn't really enjoy being pregnant. I was nauseous and vomited for the first twenty weeks or so, cursing the books that said this only lasted for twelve weeks. I did have a blooming stage between weeks twenty-eight and thirty-six, which was reflected in my skin and hair, but those last few weeks were a drag. I always found it difficult to relate my swollen stomach to the pending arrival of a baby, and the true reality did not sink in until I was at home with our one-day-old baby daughter. From the start, Tim was always hoping for a girl and his wish came true.

We are now the proud parents of Bethan Carys, and to say that she has changed our life would be the biggest understatement ever made but now, three months on, I can say that I think these changes are definitely for the better.

Andrea

* * *

OK, it's my turn now and suddenly my life does not seem nearly as exciting as everyone else's. I have never lived abroad or done anything startling that I can think of, so I might just have to make

something up if I find this gets a bit too boring. Well, I will start with the truth and see how I get on. I am twenty-nine years old and have been a police officer now for almost ten years. Fortunately I was a plain-clothes officer when I fell pregnant, because I really cannot imagine a maternity version of the uniform being particularly flattering when even the normal version would make Kate Moss look dumpy!

Being a police officer was something I always wanted to do. Ballerinas or nurses never interested me as a child – I was pretty much a tomboy from birth. The thought of breaking down doors and shouting 'You're nicked!' like they do on *The Bill* always had a certain appeal to me, so I left school at sixteen and, after working in a pet shop for two years, I signed up as soon as I hit my eighteenth birthday.

Being a tomboy, football has always been the second love of my life. I have supported Arsenal FC for as long as I can remember, along with my dad and my big brother. I also play football for the local ladies' team, where I am known for my Eric Cantona style antics, not that I have ever quite reached the point of kicking a spectator – but then again, we don't get that many spectators! Sport in general is my main hobby, both participating and spectating, and I am not just another armchair fan – I do actually go to the matches too.

I have always been a bit of a party animal. You know the sort – you show me a party and I will be there – but I have also always been teetotal, which is largely because I just do not like the taste of alcohol. So really I am the caricature of the ideal woman for most men – a woman who loves football, who would actually choose to stay in and watch *Match of the Day*, who does not drink, so can drive home after a night out. And, just to finish off this idyllic picture, my mother owns a brewery and my father owns a pub! What more could a bloke ask for? I reckon that if I had wanted to advertise myself as a potential bride I would have had them queueing up the high street!

So how did I meet my husband? Yes, you've guessed it, Bruce and I met at a football match. Not the usual romantic image of eyes meeting across a crowded room, I realize, but it worked for me! It was more a case of eyes meeting over the counter of the Gunners' Shop (which, for those of you who are not big on football, is the Arsenal souvenir shop). Nevertheless, we have not looked back since! In fact, we actually got engaged within a month of meeting each other, but decided it might be prudent to wait a whole four months before breaking the news to our families and a further twelve months before tying the knot. It was the most out of character thing I had ever done. Until then I was always Miss Sensible, weighing up the pros and cons before doing anything, and so was Bruce. So true romance can happen over a football strip, after all – so to speak!

I see that the others have told you what their husbands do for a living. Well, we have been together now for six years, and yet I don't really know what Bruce does. It is not anything particularly dodgy (which is probably just as well considering my profession) – it is just beyond my understanding. Basically, it is something to do with computers, and I am sure that is as much detail as anyone will be interested in. He runs his own business, which was definitely a bit of a plus after I had a baby, as it at least gave me a sense of security that he could be there whenever I needed him.

My family are of Greek Cypriot origin, so that will probably give you a bit of an idea of my appearance. I do have that traditional Greek look about me, complete with the excellent childbearing hips (well, that is what I like to call them, anyway). If you can conjure up the image you see on every postcard that you have received or sent from Greece of that little Greek lady wearing a black dress, knitting and herding the goats, that will be me in thirty years' time. Well, it would be me except, of course, that I cannot knit, I do not wear dresses, let alone little black dresses (the last dress I wore was on my wedding day), and if I took up goat herding in the middle-class suburbia where we live I think I would have my colleagues coming round to arrest me. So I think I will stick with kids of the human variety. Seriously though, I do have a lot of relatives who fit that image and could probably make themselves a small fortune in the postcard industry if they put their minds to it – that would help to fund feeding the goats!

With my Greek blood, it will be no surprise to know that I have always wanted babies – stacks of them! However, I still would not really class myself as the motherly type, as I'm sure you'll have picked up from this picture of me so far. I had definitely been broody for a good few years, though, but Bruce was not quite as desperate for children as I was. So when we got married he appeased me by saying we could start trying in a couple of years. Well, I held him to his word, and on our second wedding anniversary, almost to the day, I broached the subject again, and he somewhat reluctantly agreed for me to come off the Pill. We used condoms for the first three months as the books all seem to tell you. I am not entirely sure why you're meant to, but we did it anyway, and then, wham-bam, I was pregnant! I could not believe it – no thermometers or ovulation tests. We did not even make a concerted effort to find out the best time of the month. I was so excited, but poor Bruce did not really know what had hit him. He had heard that it could take up to a year after coming off the Pill, so my falling pregnant straight away knocked him for six. I kept my head down and tried to conceal my excitement until he came to terms with the big news, which fortunately did not take him too long. I do not know what it is with these men but, as with Lyndsey's husband, mine also displayed a new-found male bravado at his newly confirmed virility. I think, for Bruce, this was partly because he was adopted, which meant that he had absolutely no background knowledge of any possible hereditary conditions, so he was soon proudly boasting to everyone what good swimmers he produced and that he was no Jaffa (seedless oranges, if you are unsure of this quaint little phrase). He was so proud of his ability to father children (which of course had nothing at all to do with me and my eggs) that he even started offering his services as a sperm donor to any of my single friends who made the mistake of admitting to feelings of broodiness.

Once we had both got used to the fact that this pregnancy really was happening, Bruce actually started to get excited but, unfortunately, as his excitement increased, so did my pregnancy paranoia. You name it, I worried about it. I even worried about the effect on the baby of worrying! I worried so much, I am surprised my son Max was not born with a nervous twitch. I first started to worry when I was about six weeks pregnant and had to tell my inspector at work. This was because it was obviously no longer wise for me to go on raids or do anything dodgy like that, and 'Not tonight, I've got a headache, Sir' is not really a valid excuse in the police force. However, I started to fear that it would be tempting Fate to announce the news so early in case I had a miscarriage, so I asked the inspector to keep it quiet. Keeping something quiet in the police force is quite a unique concept. It basically means that it will take a whole twenty-four hours for the news to get around the station instead of the usual average of four hours! Mind you, once they have done the risk assessment on you, it is generally pretty obvious that something is up, since the most dangerous work they let you do is licking the stamps on the outgoing mail!

Once I had stopped worrying about miscarriage, I started worrying about disabilities, defects, death, etc. I think I must have driven poor Bruce absolutely nuts, but I have assured him that I will not be quite so paranoid by the time we get to the sixth pregnancy! If you have ever watched the Monty Python film *The Meaning of Life*, you will remember the scene where the mum with hundreds of children suddenly gives birth to yet another whilst doing the washing up, without so much as a single grunt. Well, if I have my way that is going to be me! Max was born four months ago now and we only have eyes for him at the moment. We are both absolutely besotted with him. He has totally changed our lives and, despite the negative aspects of no sleep and not going out, we cannot imagine being without him. It was a good job he was a boy, though, because if we'd had a girl I think she might have had a bit of an identity crisis. The Babygro we packed in that infamous hospital bag which sat around the house from week thirty-six was actually an Arsenal

FC one! Yes, within an hour of his birth, Max was clearly advertising his team and he has already paid a visit to Highbury, his second home. I know this might seem a little premature but he needed introducing from an early age for fear that he might be influenced at school at the age of five and, heaven forbid, start supporting Manchester United! I am afraid he would just have to leave home if that happened, so we wanted to make sure he knew his team. It is a good job that he looks good in red and white. Don't misunderstand me, there is nothing wrong with a little girl supporting football, I am living proof of this, but it would be a shame if she was ostracized from nursery because she owned an Action Man in the Arsenal kit rather than a ballerina Barbie!

Well, I don't think that I have done too badly. I have managed to write all this without having to make up a single story. I hope this gives you a bit of an idea about me and who I was before I became a mum. No, make that who I am, because I do not think that I have been changed by the motherhood experience – just expanded!

Annette

* * *

Where shall I begin? At twenty-eight years old I can proudly boast of being the youngest of our little group, although Hilary, Sarah and Andrea would hasten to add that we were all born in the same year. Isn't it funny how we all spend our early years bumping our ages up between our birthdays, but once we have passed our mid-twenties we suddenly start bumping them down and only refer to ourselves as being a year older once it would be a blatant lie not to. Please excuse this obsession with numbers, but I am an accountant by profession. I work within the male-dominated construction industry, which makes few allowances for women, let alone pregnant women and working mothers!

I grew up in a small market town, with my parents and two sisters. From a very young age I was determined to go off to university and then become a power-hungry career woman. Unfortunately, the first hurdle was my A-level grades, which were not initially up to scratch. During my final year at school, my youngest sister was very ill, and the whole family spent an anxious year with many trips to hospital, but luckily she pulled through OK. Despite my A-level setback, I was determined to find an alternative route and successfully managed to find a two-year course which would help me achieve my ambitions. So, at eighteen I left home to start a new life at college.

My first year at college was spent drinking and partying and learning essential knowledge such as how to down a pint of lager in one go. When I arrived back at college to start my second year, I promised myself I was going to focus on my work, and try to cut down on my alcohol intake. For the first three weeks I failed miserably, and even ended up in casualty after slipping over on spilt beer at a college 'beerkeller', which resulted in several stitches in my chin. The positive side of this was that it did seem to knock some sense into me, and I decided that it might be the time to look for a good man to take care of me and keep me out of trouble!

The following week I spotted Gavin across a smoky bar. For my part it was love at first sight, and a few days later the opportunity to meet face to face arose at a friend's party. I had to find a way for him to notice me, so while he was innocently trying to remember where he had left his drink, I tripped him up as he walked by and then rushed to his rescue! That was it, he was caught, and I wasn't about to let him get away.

Our relationship survived the final year of college, and then we were both lucky enough to find jobs in London, Gavin in computing and me as a trainee accountant. We initially moved into separate house-shares, but a year later Gavin moved in with me. I was not quite sure how my mum and dad would take to me living in sin, so I decided to wait until the time was right before announcing this fact. The matter was unfortunately taken out of my hands, however, when my dad paid a surprise visit one Saturday and Gavin had just done his washing. All his underpants were very neatly laid out on the radiators in the lounge, so there was no hiding it! My dad politely didn't comment, but I could tell that he found it all mildly entertaining – luckily!

Once we had been found out, we decided to make our situation slightly more permanent by buying a flat together. During this time I was studying for my accountancy exams, so Gavin became the proper little house husband, cooking all the meals and doing all the housework to give me maximum studying time. Not wishing to lose this domesticated darling I would sometimes broach the subject of marriage, but Gavin would steadfastly inform me that he never wanted to marry.

Three and a half years after leaving college, I had passed all my exams, and with Gavin still doing all the domestic chores I then had a lot more time on my hands – more thinking time – more thinking-about-getting-married time! Gavin still stubbornly vowed that he did not want to marry, but I decided to stand my ground, and gave him six months to make his final decision. Just before the six months were up, Gavin announced that he had two weeks off work the following February and said, 'I suppose we could use this for a honeymoon!' Not a very romantic proposal, I realize, but a proposal none the less. Gavin did not want a large wedding and this had formed a great part of his lack of desire to get married, so I willingly agreed to have a small wedding, and between us we formulated a master plan.

Our parents had never met, so we arranged for them to meet on neutral territory in a pub. Gavin then made a formal announcement that we were to be married, and both lots of parents dutifully and excitedly congratulated us. The real shock came for them when they asked when the big day would be, only to find out that it was in fifteen minutes' time! I will always remember the look of happiness on their faces, shortly followed by the look of shock, shortly followed by the look of total disbelief. We immediately ordered a quick celebratory drink before heading for the registry office. The weeks of silent preparation had paid off and they had not suspected a thing. My dad still has fond memories of the following week, when he kept talking to himself out loud, trying to make sense of it, and although as a child I had had the usual fairy-tale dreams of a big white wedding, my small, red-clad wedding was still the best day of my life.

We then decided that we had had enough of living in London and wanted to live somewhere quieter where the neighbours were friendly and the air was clean. So we moved to our current home, an old Edwardian property in need of much repair. The next year and a half was spent decorating and taking rubble to the local dump.

At this time I was still travelling into London to a job which I enjoyed, both socially and in terms of climbing up the career ladder. Gavin was keen to start a family but I was still a little hesitant, although I was gradually coming round to the idea. Once we had both decided to try for a family, I was unsure whether I would be able to cope with being both pregnant and a London commuter, until one day my mind was made up for me when I sat next to a pregnant woman on the train. She looked uncomfortable in the small seat on the crowded train, and when we pulled into Euston station she turned a strange colour and promptly threw up everywhere. All the men close by, including my husband, legged it, leaving me 'holding the baby', so to speak, as I helped this poor woman clean herself up. So that was that – I changed jobs to avoid a similar incident happening to me.

I stopped taking the Pill in February, but we were careful until August, when we started trying seriously for a baby. I bought a water-sample test to work out my most fertile time, only to find that we had missed it! Therefore in the September, to avoid this happening again, we *really* went for it and fortunately we hit the jackpot! We were both delighted when I missed a period and the pregnancy test showed a positive result. I don't think either of us could have endured another such active month. It made the *Gladiators* eliminator round seem like a walk in the park!

After the initial excitement of being pregnant, I went through a period of emotional turmoil. I was worried about my pending new responsibilities as a mother, and I was worried about the unborn child's health. My mother had given birth to four children, but only two had survived. The most recent tragedy was my youngest sister, who had been diagnosed as having a rare genetic disorder at a very young age, and had died less than a year ago. I had grown up watching her gradually deteriorate, and the memories of this were deeply engrained, so naturally I was worried in case history repeated itself. I was sent to see various consultants, who all reassured me that the chances of my child having the disease were slim – one in six hundred. However, there were no specific tests that could be done, so I had to try and put my concerns to one side.

I am not sure when pregnancy seemed a reality. When we had the first scan at three months, it was exciting, but still not real. After this scan, we shared the news with friends and relatives, but again it still did not feel real. When I was twenty-two weeks pregnant, I was at work one day when I suddenly experienced severe chest pains which brought tears to my eyes. I was immediately sent to the doctor and then to casualty, where a suspected blood clot was diagnosed. I remember feeling absolutely terrified. Phoning Gavin at work, I tried desperately to sound calm so as not to panic him, but tears got the better of me. He could have knocked spots off Damon Hill's best lap time with the speed he got to the hospital! It was St Valentine's Day, definitely the worst St Valentine's Day we have ever had. I was so frightened that I had done something stupid to put my unborn child's health at risk, and because I was wound up, I couldn't feel the baby kicking at all, so this upset me even more. But once I had calmed down I felt movement, and I knew that if I rested and did everything the doctors said we should be OK. I was released a week later, fully rested and fully recovered.

The blood clot brought home to me the fact that I was nurturing a little living person inside me, and pregnancy did feel more real after that, but it was not until I gave birth to Emily Louise that all my anxieties were relieved. I will never forget Gavin saying to me when he first saw her, 'She's perfect.'

When people used to say to me that having a baby had changed their lives for the better, I quite honestly did not believe them. But it is so true. I loved being pregnant, and I love being a mother. I cannot remember what life was like before, now, but I definitely do not want it to change. My career ambitions have now slipped to a low second place.

In terms of Emily's health, she is doing well. I watch her every day for signs of my sister's illness, and I can tell my parents do the same whenever they see her, but so far, so good. What I do see is a little person who is happy, headstrong and always hungry! I cannot think who she takes after . . .

Back to School – Antenatal Classes

The NHS antenatal classes were where the five of us first met, so we thought that this would be the best starting point for our book, but also probably the dodgiest, as this is where we reveal what we really thought of each other in the beginning.

The classes were divided into two blocks. The early parenting classes took place around the sixteen to eighteen-week mark and were designed for both parents to attend. The five of us were somehow divided between three groups for these classes, so we did not get to know each other until the second block. These took place when everyone was about thirty weeks and involved six daytime sessions for the prospective mothers, with one evening session at the end for both parents. There were twenty-four women in our group, but somehow the five of us emerged from this as a smaller antenatal group and, more importantly, postnatal group of our very own.

There is definitely a bizarre element to attending antenatal classes. After all, there is very little you actually learn at them that most people would not have read in a book. So a whole room full of ever-expanding women, sitting around with the only real thing in common between them being their stomachs, definitely has a comical element to it.

When the five of us spent an evening discussing this chapter and what our vivid memories were from the antenatal classes, it was amazing to hear that we all had unsavoury thoughts about what we'd had to do and about the other people in the sessions. Yet we had all talked nicely to everyone and politely done the exercises, without any hint of objection at the time.

We realize now that the structure of the classes was actually a cunning ploy on the part of the midwife running them. To take part in such bizarre activities is a guaranteed way to encourage camaraderie, and strong friendships were built from this. The greatest thing you can gain from any antenatal group has to be the knowledge that you have friends out there going through the same postnatal experiences as you, at the same time, and for this essential survival provision we applaud the success of the antenatal classes.

Hilary

* * *

I attended antenatal classes with the sole aim of finding other people on a similar wavelength to me who would be having a baby at the same time. The prospect of being at home all day, every day, without any company except 'the blob' was so frightening that I was determined to find a companion to get through this with.

I had been warned that earth mother types tended to go to the private antenatal classes, which partners attend too. However, I could not even begin to envisage me, let alone David, sitting in a circle of pregnant couples on floor cushions puffing and panting to whale music, as the books always seem to depict, so I decided that these classes were not going to be for me.

I had been told by friends that the NHS classes would be full of teenage single mums and that I would probably end up practising my newly acquired mothering skills on them rather than learning anything for myself at the group, but I decided to give these a go, at least. Initially we signed up for three evening sessions for both parents, and to my total amazement David agreed to attend. As the date for the first session approached, he began to panic about the fact that he was a sheep farmer and lambing was about to start. We had read so much about toxoplasmosis and how important it is for pregnant women to stay well away from pregnant sheep, that David thought that at the first

*David thought that at the first mention of his job the whole
room would evacuate*

mention of his job the whole room would evacuate, leaving the
two of us apologizing to the midwife for the sudden reduction
in group size. He made me promise not to mention what he
farmed, and then all the way there in the car he was saying things
like, 'If you so much as *mention* sheep I'm leaving.'

Well, we got there and sat in silence, along with all the other
couples, waiting for someone to speak. Then, much to David's
horror, the first task issued by the midwife running the session
was for us all to introduce ourselves and say what we did. David
went first, and being an absolutely lousy liar instantly blurted out,

'My name is David and I am a sheep farmer!' It was a bit like a first-time attendee at an Alcoholics Anonymous meeting standing up and admitting that he was an alcoholic. I almost expected a round of applause to follow for his admission to such an affliction. We never did establish whether it was down to ignorance or politeness that this had no effect on the group, but apart from constant references to his ability to deliver the baby feet-first himself, we somehow got away without being ostracized.

This was not quite the case for David at home, who was banished from our house for the whole of lambing. I made the poor chap strip down to his boxer shorts outside and get in the shower every time he so much as thought about coming into the house. It was a bit like one of those nuclear power station cleansing units, but without the sirens and flashing lights.

The second set of classes started when I was twenty-five weeks, and having had no contact with any pregnant women since the previous classes, I was determined not to come out at the end of these ones being a Billy No Mates, so I tackled them with a new-found air of confidence. Unfortunately, I was late for the first session, which meant that instead of being able to size up who looked worth talking to, I had to take the only seat left, between the woman who looked like a librarian and the 'Aren't I little and cute with a high-pitched voice' woman. Well, to say that these two were not on my wavelength is putting it extremely mildly – Captain Charisma they were not. We were divided into groups of three and left to discuss our fears and thoughts on our pregnancies. Well, usually I would see that as an opportunity to have a good getting-to-know-you type chat, as I am sure was intended – but not us. We drew up a list of questions we wanted answering, such as: 'What sort of dosage of pethidine is given and how long until it takes effect? At what stage does the foetus develop eyes? How much fluid should we take in each day during pregnancy? The only question I could think of to contribute was, How do you stop yourself from pooing in labour? But I realized that this was not going to go down very well with my more serious companions, so I kept it to myself. Don't get me wrong, all their questions were perfectly valid and I probably wanted to know the answers to them as well at some point, but just not in the getting-to-know-you gossip time. I kept looking longingly at the other little groups all chatting away and hoping a sense of humour would suddenly leap out of my two companions and smack me in the face like the Orange Tango glove! But it never came.

The second week was not much better. This time we had to do a breathing exercise with our neighbour. Again I was late, and ended up sitting next to a lady who was so thin she looked as though her legs would snap. The exercise involved one person holding the other's wrist and gradually squeezing it harder and harder. The person being squeezed had to pretend that this was a contraction and breathe their way through it. I have never been big on body contact with casual acquaintances, so I really did not fancy this. I had also eaten garlic the night before, so did not think that my partner would really want to be subjected to me developing an over-zealous fake contraction, as this was more likely to anaesthetize her with the stench of garlic than help me deal with pain. But she seemed keen to have a go and I could see no escape. While everyone else prepared themselves, sitting straddling chairs or on all fours, I went to the loo in a desperate attempt to put off the inevitable. But having seen how keen my companion was to do the exercise, guilt got the better of me and I returned with just enough time for only one of us to do it. In order to save her from my garlic breath, I suggested that she did the breathing while I squeezed her wrist. What I failed to consider was that spindle-legs lady also had spindle wrists and that I, with my history of many triumphs in arm-wrestling competitions, did not know my own strength. The poor girl genuinely had to breathe her way through the pain, and although she did not say anything afterwards, I did notice her rubbing her wrist for the rest of the session and she never sat next to me again!

With these two sessions under my belt, I did not feel that I had made much progress in my quest to gain friends. Fortunately, I made sure I arrived early enough in future sessions to choose my seating a little more selectively, and gradually our little gaggle of like-minded girlies got together.

The one disadvantage I had with our group was the fact that I was the last one due to give birth. At first I thought this was a big plus, as it meant I could pick all my new-found friends' brains throughout my pregnancy as to what to expect to happen next. This has been the case since Molly was born, too. I have had four experts to get advice from – because, believe me, four weeks' advance experience in newborn baby terms definitely qualifies you as an expert. However, waiting for the big day was a complete nightmare, because as each of the others gradually left the land of pregnancy and entered the new world of motherhood, the panic in me increased. I just could not relate to them once they had joined the club that I was not yet a member of. When it got down to just me and Lyndsey, I had to put her on my BT Friends and Family scheme because my phone bill was so high! Then when Lyndsey joined the motherhood club, leaving me alone for nearly two more weeks in my paranoid world of pregnancy, I thought it would never happen! The other reason I became so panicky was because I had read so many facts and figures about complications in childbirth. One in five will have this, one in ten will have that, and so on. The others all seemed to have had perfectly normal deliveries, with straightforward labours and healthy babies. So as far as I was concerned, this left me destined for a three-day labour finished off by a Caesarean, due to a breach baby which had something wrong with it to boot! Fortunately, my paranoia was unfounded and I eventually joined the motherhood club with no complications at all.

Sarah

* * *

There was some confusion over my invitation to the early parenting classes, so by the time I eventually turned up at them I was already six months pregnant. I found it rather amusing that the majority of ladies present ranged from fifteen to eighteen weeks and seemed to be looking at me, with my bonny twenty-four-week bump, as some kind of an expert. It was as though they believed that the bigger the stomach, the more motherly instinct you possessed! To make me stand out even more, I was also the only one there who was without a partner. Tim was out in Spain all week so he could not attend the Monday-evening classes. At the time, I thought my imagination was running riot, but I swore I could see the others sizing me up. I was squirming in my seat at the notion that the group was pigeon-holing me as a single mother, and I desperately wanted to stand up and say, 'I have got a husband.'

My paranoid self-consciousness, I discovered later, was not entirely unfounded. Hilary's husband, David, had satisfied his boredom throughout these sessions by making up scenarios for the lives of everyone there. Apparently he had me down as a lesbian who had obtained her six-foot-dark-haired-rocket-scientist sperm from the sperm bank and had it artificially inseminated by her lover, who had since left her for an animal-rights campaigner. Suddenly the single-mother label seems positively appealing.

I found the antenatal classes to be a unique experience. I have always been quite a self-confident person, who finds opening conversation with new acquaintances relatively easy. Yet attending these classes was reminiscent of the first day at school at the age of five. Everyone appeared to be seeking refuge behind their partners, as a child would behind its mother's coat, and no couples spoke to anyone else. All the men appeared to be encouraging their wives to speak up and mingle with the other ladies in a fatherly way. 'Off you go and talk to the other children – I am sure they are very friendly!' In the meantime, the women were all sussing each other out, trying to decide whether or not anyone was worth making an effort to talk to. 'She looks a bit of a laugh, and she isn't afraid to ask daft questions like me, so perhaps I'll talk to her at the coffee break. I'll give her a smile and see how she responds. No, I don't think she wants to know, stuck-up cow! What about her next-door neighbour? She looks a bit too sensible, I expect she will only want to talk about sterilizers and the latest in nappy design.' And so the thought process went on. Well, that is how my brain was working, anyway. It's strange how, when you've reached a mature enough age to be expecting a baby yourself, you still act as if you're in kindergarten!

One of the things that has astounded me most is that the five of us who built a close friendship out of the antenatal class are such diverse characters. The only thing we really all have in common is our babies, yet we pride ourselves on the fact that they are not our sole topic of conversation and that our friendship exists despite, not because of, them. The difference between Andrea and me in particular was highlighted for me when we met one day and Max was wearing his red and white Arsenal shirt. I hasten to add at this point that football has never been an interest of mine in any shape or form, so I commented on what a good quality shirt it was and enquired as to whether they were also made in navy or black. I honestly had no idea that different football teams had their own strip, but I was soon educated in this matter by a horrified Andrea. It is amazing what you learn through the experience of childbirth!

Tim did manage to be in the country for one of the later-session fathers' evenings, much to my relief, but one thing I failed to mention earlier is that Tim is not the sort of chap who likes to fade into the background in any situation. As a rule, centre stage is where he is most comfortable. This often leaves me wanting to run to the wings with embarrassment. Well, this evening was to be no exception. The session was run by one of the health visitors, whose presentation skills and personality could only politely be described as bland. She was wearing a nylon suit comprising a turquoise waistcoat with white-stitched trim and a matching A-line skirt. This ensemble was complemented by a rather fetching white ruffled blouse, which resulted in a close resemblance to a cross between Mrs Merton and Dick Turpin. She then proceeded to provide the group with some painfully boring facts, which she presented in a monotonous voice whilst peering over her half-moon glasses. She ended her little introduction by giving a description of her absent health-visitor colleague, so that all present would recognize who she was when they did get to meet her. This description was by no means flattering, since she referred to her colleague as having grey hair, big glasses, a quiet Scottish accent and very short legs. At this point I could see Tim preparing himself for his first contribution to the evening, and before I could stop him he had leapt in with, 'She sounds lovely, Shirley, but please do tell us, how does she describe you?' This comment resulted in a decidedly pinched look appearing on Shirley's face and the rest of the group tittering like schoolchildren, but left me fearing that our child's future health care had just been thrust into jeopardy as a result of its father's naughty-schoolboy attitude.

Being away a lot of the time, Tim had taken very little interest in the pregnancy. This had been a bit of a bugbear for me, because I felt he could have at least attempted for my sake to read up on the subject. Well, after his attendance at this fathers' evening, I really had to eat my words. The final part of the evening took the format of a quiz, involving a list of questions on labour. Tim then proceeded to live up to his new-found reputation of 'clever dick' by being the only man present who was able to answer all of the questions correctly. The few seconds spent looking over my shoulder in bed, whilst I was poring over

Miriam Stoppard's *Conception, Pregnancy and Birth*, had obviously paid off.

I do not know exactly what I did gain from attending these antenatal classes other than a reputation for having a smart arse as a husband and, of course, the friendship of the rest of this gang. But, to be quite honest, that in itself was plenty. Unfortunately, Tim could only come home for five days around the time of Jack's birth, so my antenatal buddies became my lifeline to sanity in those early weeks, which is something I will never forget.

Andrea

***

I was really such a miserable old bag throughout all of the antenatal classes that I cannot think why I bothered attending them at all. As I work in the town I live in, I was petrified that I might end up in the same group as someone I had previously arrested, but fortunately that didn't happen. Despite this, I still did not want to partake in any of the activities or talk to any of the other people present. I must have made Victor Meldrew look like a total pussycat, so I am surprised that I managed to come out of these sessions with even one friend, let alone four!

The first antenatal hurdle I had to leap was when I received my letter inviting me to the early parenting classes. The sticking point of this invitation was the wording, which actually said 'you and your partner'. I knew that there was absolutely no way that Bruce was going to attend willingly. I tried bribery, I tried begging and I even tried the promise of sexual favours, but eventually I conceded that I was fighting a losing battle and that Bruce was not going to accompany me. I really did not want to go on my own, so I asked my best friend Lizzie to come with me, which she did willingly. I was really grateful for her companionship, as this really was a 'Mr and Mrs' event, and I am only grateful that Hilary was not at the same early parenting classes as me, because David would have had an absolute field day with his life-scenario game on Lizzie and me!

After sizing up the group at the first of these sessions, I decided that I had absolutely nothing in common with any of them and that I would not return. Lizzie, however, had different ideas! She found the whole thing mildly entertaining and persuaded me to give it a second chance. When we arrived the following week we were early, which is pretty much par for the course with me. There was only one other lady there and, much to my delight, she was partnerless! I made an instant bee-line for this lonesome soul, who turned out to be Annette, and our friendship was instantly cemented. Lizzie's services were no longer required after this, which was quite fortunate, because just the two sessions had been enough to put her off having children for life! She said that merely hearing the horror stories of morning sickness and weight gain was the most effective form of contraception she had ever come across.

I attended the last of these early sessions with Annette and, with the encouragement of my new-found buddy, I decided to be a total glutton for punishment and endure the second set of classes. The attraction of these was, I must admit, the prospect of six afternoons off work, as much tea and as many biscuits as I could possibly consume, all for the bargain price of ten pence, and the opportunity to catch up on a bit of sleep with an afternoon snooze afterwards. Looking back now, I realize that my understanding of the purpose of these classes may have been somewhat ill-founded, so it will be no surprise to know that I found the exercises we had to endure extremely irritating and farcical. These exercises were obviously meant to be the purpose of the classes, and the majority of people present had attended specifically for them and *not* for the biscuits, but I was determined to maintain my miserable Meldrew attitude throughout!

Hilary made reference to *everyone* sitting on cushions or strad-dling chairs for the wrist-squeezing exercise. I would like to clarify that while she was hiding in the toilet, I was refusing

point-blank to straddle anything, and the unfortunate girl part-
nered with me had the shortest contraction in history. She did
not even have time to catch her breath once before it was over
and I was sitting back with my arms folded declaring that we had
finished!

On another occasion, we were put into small groups and given
some cut-out pictures of baby equipment which we then had to
stick on to a piece of paper under either the heading 'essential'
or 'desirable'. I think the midwife must have been trying to pad
out the session because we were given fifteen minutes to decide
the fate of only six items, none of which required much thought
or deliberation. Our group, led by me, managed to complete this
task in less than fifteen seconds. I have not actually had the desire
to do cutting and pasting since I was about five and no hidden
pleasure in this activity was about to emerge. As we had items
such as nappies and baby clothes to deliberate over, you can
imagine that discussion was kept to a minimum, leaving our
group with plenty of time to get another cup of tea and more
biscuits, while we waited for the other groups to complete the
task. I cannot imagine to this day how they managed to stretch
out a discussion for so long on whether nappies are essential or
desirable. All I could think was that if they did not know the
answer by now, they were in for a terrible shock once their
babies were born!

Despite all these activities, I must say that I did enjoy the
classes, although this was largely because of Fiona the midwife,
who was a great source of entertainment. For some reason, Fiona
found it impossible to let any of the six sessions go by without at
least one viewing of her knickers. Unbeknown to her, she soon
earned herself the nickname of Flash Your Knickers Fiona, as we
took bets each week on how many minutes into the session it
would be before we received the first viewing. Fortunately, I
took up my weekly seating position at the top end of the room,
which meant that although I could make an appraisal of her latest
underwear I was not in the full gynaecological viewing zone. I

only discovered just how unfortunate a position those seated at the bottom end of the room were in when during one session Annette felt faint and left the room. When she returned she was greeted with a full view of Flash Your Knickers Fiona's demonstration of the final stage of labour, skirt hitched up, and not just her knickers but most of their contents also clearly on display to half of the room! Annette's face was an absolute picture – her eyes expanded to twice their original size, then she went pale and made a beeline for the toilet. Each week without fail an opportunity arose and up went Fiona's skirt. At one point she even shoved a doll up her frock and did a performance of the full labour process from first contraction through to delivery. She had definitely missed out on her true vocation in life as an actress.

Well, despite my porcupine-like approach to these classes, I have to say how glad I was that I persevered with them. I came out with four new friends, I got my money's worth of NHS biscuits and enough knowledge on the wide range of knickers available on the British market to have enabled me to write a survey for *Which* magazine.

Annette

***

I attended my first set of antenatal classes at sixteen weeks. I was quite relieved that the NHS were running courses because I had heard from a friend that she was set homework at the private courses. This instantly conjured up the image of me wading my way through childbirth textbooks and doing presentations on flip charts or overhead projectors to the rest of the group each week, which was all way beyond my level of interest in the pending birth.

The first set of NHS antenatal classes were held over three evenings. Having missed the first night due to being late home from work, I was in two minds as to whether to attend the others at all. To add to this dilemma, Gavin had arranged for a builder to come round to discuss quotes, and so if I was going to go, I would be going alone. After some deliberation, though, I decided that if I was going to be a mother, I should not be such a wimp and should attend anyway.

I thought it would be a good idea to arrive first so that I could eye everyone up as they arrived. The first people to enter the room were Andrea and Lizzie and I thought, 'Great – two other women without husbands. This will not be as bad as I originally thought!' However, I managed to put my foot in it big time by commenting to Lizzie that she had a very neat bump, only to find out that she was not actually pregnant at all, and was only there to keep Andrea company. Unfortunately a huge hole in the ground didn't appear and swallow me up as I hoped it would, but Andrea and Lizzie were kind enough to laugh off my enormous blunder.

Having survived the evening and actually quite enjoyed it, I looked forward to the last session, for which I arranged to meet Andrea again, as the only other manless woman. To my surprise, though, Gavin volunteered to attend and, not wishing to offend him (after all he *was* the father), I agreed for him to come along. Unfortunately, Andrea had turned up without Lizzie, having gained confidence from my lonesome presence the week before. She took one look at Gavin and remarked, 'Huh, what is *he* doing here?' Gavin felt so uncomfortable that he ended up being more like the single parent for the evening than Andrea.

The rest of the evening was spent playing with the baby resuscitation doll. We learnt how to dress and undress it and change nappies. Finally, we were taught baby resuscitation techniques, which felt very peculiar. Here we were, pregnant, not even having a living baby yet, and we were learning how to bring a baby back to life! There was a small incident when Gavin blew too hard into the baby's mouth and the chest nearly exploded. This at least confirmed the need to practise this skill on a doll rather than on a real baby. Towards the end of the evening Andrea seemed to forgive me for bringing Gavin along, and we agreed to meet up again and go to aqua-aerobics together.

The next set of antenatal classes were on six Monday afternoons. By this time, Andrea and I were meeting up regularly to go swimming. We decided to meet on Monday lunchtimes too and go out for lunch before each class. I could hardly believe my luck – another pregnant woman who loved her food!

There was a wide variety of people at these classes, and it was a long afternoon if you ended up sitting next to the wrong person, which happened to me on a couple of occasions. Several times we were split into small groups to discuss different subjects, and we then had to nominate a team leader to present our discussion. For some reason I always seemed to manage to get into a group with the long-blonde-haired Scandinavians who did not appear to speak much English. This meant that not only were our discussions kept to a minimum, with me speaking in a slow deliberate manner all the time, but also that being one of the only fluent-English-speaking members of the group, I always seemed to be nominated to do the presentations. To think that I had avoided the private classes for this very reason! On one occasion, I managed to draw the shortest possible straw and got in a group with all three of the Scandinavian-looking women. Having done my usual 'I'm conversing with foreigners' explanation to them of what we were meant to be doing, I suddenly noticed the smirk on the third blonde's face. This long-haired blonde turned out to be 'Geordie' Lyndsey, who does not have an ounce of Nordic blood in her. She was extremely polite and patient with the other team members, but I could read from her facial expression that she was on the same wavelength as me. The Scandinavians were very nice, but at the end of the day it is not easy to get a good girlie giggle going on subjects such as deteriorating sex lives and expanding boobs with someone for whom you have to translate every word into textbook English.

By the third week, I had established who I had absolutely

nothing in common with and did not want to spend the afternoon sitting next to, and I would arrive early to find a suitable seat. It was then a matter of playing the eye-contact game. As each person arrived, I would desperately try to avoid eye contact with the people I had nothing in common with, in order to discourage them from sitting next to me. Childish, I realize, but believe me, it was necessary! If this antic failed to work, then I had to resort to going to the loo or feeling faint, as an excuse to surreptitiously leave the room and re-enter some time later, hoping that someone had taken my original seat thus freeing me to sit elsewhere. Little did I know that Hilary was playing the same game!

The two things that I really wanted to learn from the classes were relaxation and the technique of breathing through contractions. Friends kept telling me that it was very important to grasp this skill in order to help me deal with pain through labour. At the time it seemed as though Flash Your Knickers Fiona was skimming over this subject, concentrating more on her pants of the lacy variety than our pants of the breathing variety. But as it turned out, she did in fact teach us all there is to know. When the chips are down in the throes of labour, you pant for England.

I was quite concerned that Gavin would not know what to expect when I went into labour, so, in a desperate attempt to ensure that he did not escape the last fathers' evening by arranging another convenient appointment with a builder, I had described Flash Your Knickers Fiona to him as a twenty-five-year-old, long-legged sexy babe, who flashed her silky lingerie at every available opportunity. I just could not keep him away after that description! He was a little disappointed, to say the least, when he did see Fiona, in her early fifties, slightly overweight, with varicose veins, and he was actually relieved that she was wearing trousers when she started her legs-spread demos! I was amazed at how much Gavin already knew as well. He certainly did not need to attend for educational purposes, which made my detailed deception to get him there seem quite obsolete. At the end of the day he learnt nothing, talked to nobody and did not even get to see a babe's knickers, as promised!

Lyndsey

* * *

I also attended the antenatal classes with some trepidation. My main fear was that the average age of the others was going to be about twenty-four and that I would be the oldest in the group. I was pleasantly surprised, therefore, to find that the majority of the women in our group were in their late twenties or early thirties and that I wasn't an old hen at all. In fact I was positively youthful compared to some of the others, who looked as though they were ready to draw their pensions rather than child benefit! Once that hurdle was over, I had to admit that I enjoyed the camaraderie of the group. It was great to be finally sitting in a room full of women who knew exactly how I felt and could sympathize with the useless male element of pregnant life. Tim tried his hardest to be sympathetic, but was the first to admit that it wasn't quite the same for him as it was for me and therefore could not drum up much excitement when, for example, I felt a flutter in my stomach. Was it the baby or was it my bowels? It was so difficult to tell in those early months. He dutifully, albeit begrudgingly, agreed to attend one fathers' evening, but he was in a little world of his own as the midwife went into a detailed and prolonged description of the importance of using relaxation techniques to keep your partner calm during the long hours of labour. I thought he seemed uncharacteristically interested as she demonstrated various techniques and soon discovered why. After the full demo, he turned to me and without hesitation said, 'That's excellent, I hope you took that all in because I really think that I might need them when it gets to the gory bit. She's right, I'll probably find it a bit stressful.' I promptly pointed out that it was *him* who was supposed to be keeping *me* relaxed, and then started to doubt whether he was going to be the perfect birthing partner, let alone father! But it has to be said that once the baby was born, Tim was a star, and any signs of disinterest that had been present before the birth immediately vanished.

One big advantage of attending the classes was to get some idea of maternity wear. I quickly came to the conclusion that the high-street shops and even the specialist shops and catalogues are either not geared to the growing figure, or offered grotesquely shaped clothes made from disgusting material. As we were a big group, I found myself taking more notice of the clothes than the names, and it seems I was not the only one, because as the five of us chatted, in later weeks, we politely referred to the rest of the group by their attire rather than their names – 'the girl in the lime Lycra dress' or 'the girl in the track suit'. It amazed me what some women would wear, irrespective of the stage of pregnancy or the season. Because of this fascination with fatty fashion, and because I'm the last to go in this chapter, you've already had the details of the classes, so I have been given the bitchy task of giving some details about the more colourful characters of the antenatal group, who will probably feature in later stories.

First of all there was Ms Textbook. I think there must be one in every group – she was the one who had read a book on everything. Whatever the subject, she knew all about it. She knew every fact and figure, every pro and con, and even put the poor midwife running the session to shame on a couple of occasions. If I had been running the class, I reckon I would have just handed over to her saying, 'Well, you are obviously the expert so please do take over!' Just to add to the irritation, she also had quite a bizarre appearance. I think the last time she actually purchased any clothing was in about 1980. She wore Lady Diana ruff-necked blouses and pleated skirts every single week, and although they altered slightly in style, they all seemed to be in varying shades of beige. We never did ascertain her exact age, but our estimations ranged from a very untrendy

thirty-year-old to an equally untrendy forty-five-plus. Her husband was equally bizarre in appearance and seemed to have got
stuck in the same time warp. Isn't it brilliant how there is someone
for everyone? You can imagine, then, my absolute horror when,
during one session, Ms Textbook embarked on a lengthy solil-
oquy on her fears of her breasts losing their sexuality through
breastfeeding. This instantly conjured up in my mind the unwel-
come image of Mr Beige Lurch Man lustfully gnawing on Ms
Textbook's nipples which, believe you me, was an image I
desperately did not want to stay with for long.

Next there was Lime Lycra Lady, who appeared to be on a
mission to demonstrate just how much stretch Lycra really does
have. The first week she came, her lime-green Lycra dress was a
pretty snug fit, but she wore the same frock every week. I accept
that it may have been comfortable to wear with all that stretchy
fabric, but enough is enough – the rest of the world could watch
as her tummy button gradually changed from its inward resting
place to outward protrusion as the weeks passed by.

This snug fit was a total contrast to Kaftan Queen, who
was your earth mother type. Everything she wore was flowing,
shapeless and tie-dyed, similar to Sarah's attire in her teenage
years, and she seemed obsessed with aromatherapy and environ-
mentally friendly nappies. She hired a home birthing pool and
arranged for her belly-dancing buddies to come round and help
her deal with labour – don't ask me how! Apparently, whale
music, warm water and wobbling bellies were her chosen
methods of managing in labour, which were a million miles away
from my preferred methods of TENS, pethidine, gas and air,
more pethidine and, if necessary, a tad more pethidine.

Finally, the Local Yokel was about as different from these girls
as is possible. She spoke in a country-bumpkin-type accent. To
me, she seemed the epitome of the farmer's wife – far more so
than Hilary will ever be. She wore a black pinafore dress from
the start of her pregnancy right to the end; I imagine she probably
gave birth in it! Initially, as it was winter, she wore a white

sweater under the pinafore, but as spring approached this was replaced with a white blouse, and then with a white T-shirt. I was just glad she gave birth before the summer weather really kicked in or I think she would have come along just wearing a bra underneath! She seemed to be the sort of woman who was so enthused with her new-found state of pregnancy that you could picture her thrusting out her bloated stomach from about ten weeks and stroking her belly, which contained nothing bigger than a broad bean, as though she was in the third trimester. When I met people like that at the early parenting classes, waddling around and complaining about the lack of sleep due to the size of the bump, I wondered how they would possibly cope when they really did hit the big time and, more importantly, how their partners would cope.

Andrea was the only member of our little group who earned herself a nickname due to her attire. She was soon renamed Alkie, due to the fact that she always wore brewery sweatshirts or T-shirts. I had her down as being a serious drinker, which just goes to show how deceptive first impressions can be, since she is in fact teetotal! I am just glad that I did not mention that I had a Ph.D. in those early weeks, as the rest of the gang have now reliably informed me that they certainly wouldn't have befriended me, but would have put me in the boffin box and closed the lid for good!

Boobs – from Bee Stings to Beach Balls

It is hard to believe just how obsessive a subject boobs can be during pregnancy. For most women, once you have grown them, they are just something stuck on your front that you either cover up or flaunt according to the situation or your personality, without really giving them too much thought. For blokes, they are an object of sexuality and therefore a subject of fascination and male-bonding-type discussions. From puberty and even earlier, boys enjoy exhausting the subject of size, angle, nipple colour and so on, with monotonous regularity, and they never really seem to grow out of this childish hobby.

So when your boobs suddenly start changing to take on their primary function of feeding, this is definitely a huge change for all involved! I mean, once you know your boobs are full of milk, do you want a bloke touching them, let alone kissing and caressing them? Some women may find this sensual, but others definitely just feel like the Unigate milkman for babies!

The prospect of a baby sucking on your nipple is a difficult one to grasp, which I think is partly why the changes to the boobs are so fascinating. For most of us, the prospect of owning a baby was a difficult enough concept to grasp, but having another human (other than your partner), and one you don't even know yet, sucking on your breasts was definitely beyond the realms of most of our imaginations.

Watching the videos on breastfeeding at the antenatal classes brought home just how alien a concept this was. We women were all able to endure watching these educational videos, although I think we all felt fairly daunted by the fast-approaching reality they showed. The faces on all of the men, however, were an absolute picture! The poor chaps did not know how to react.

After all, there is nothing more alien than blokes watching videos containing boobs without being able to convey either of the two responses – sexual or amused – which they seem to be trained to give from birth. The way the expectant fathers watched, with such serious expressions of concentration, anyone would think they had all turned into gynaecologists overnight!

Well, boobs – expanding, shrinking, feeding, not feeding, leaking, not leaking – you name it, we have experienced it!

Annette

* * *

One of the best things about the whole pregnancy and mother-hood experience for me was having bigger boobs! I am proud to say that I started off as an A cup and finished up sporting a rather pleasant B cup. When I began to breastfeed, I nearly reached the dizzy heights of a C cup, but it wasn't meant to be. I loved my new-found bursting cleavage and so did Gavin. I was so delighted with this that I was tempted to feed Emily until she was old enough to leave home, in order to preserve my B cup for another eighteen years or so. Emily, I'm sure, would have a whole different opinion on that issue.

I was always determined to breastfeed and so I deliberately refrained from purchasing any bottles or sterilizing equipment in order to ensure that I persevered with the breast. As it happened, though, Emily was born to breastfeed – she absolutely loved it. I was always a little shy about the prospect of public feeding, but during the first few weeks I was very pleased to discover how easy it was to do this discreetly. I would put Emily on a boob and guests didn't even seem to know that I was feeding her. This was particularly highlighted when Bruce and Andrea visited two days after the birth. I was breastfeeding when they came in and Bruce just stared straight at my boob and started making all the usual dutiful comments about how sweet Emily looked. He had no idea what I was doing and his face was an absolute picture when I stopped halfway to switch boobs. It was only then that it hit the poor man that it had appeared as though he had been ogling my breasts and not admiring my baby at all! If Bruce had visited a couple of weeks later, however, he would have been in no doubt at all about what was occurring. Just when I had developed the confidence to feed Emily discreetly in any circumstances, she decided to develop some extremely antisocial table manners. The guzzling, gulping, sucking and lip-smacking sounds which emerged at full volume from my chest left absolutely nothing to the imagination. It sounded like the soundtrack from a very cheap porno movie, which unfortunately had the devastating effect of causing the spotlight to turn straight on us whenever I breastfed.

I also earned the nickname of Mrs Notepad from Andrea during my breastfeeding spell, because in the early weeks I always carried a notepad with me to record which boob I had just fed from, and for how long Emily had fed. Wherever we were, out shopping or visiting friends, my notepad would appear. I think it is a first-time-mother thing. I feel sure that when I have my second child I will be much more blasé about it all and you never know, I may even stretch to allowing the baby a whole thirty seconds longer on one breast than the other!

I always knew that I would be returning to work when Emily was three months old, so I tried to introduce her to a bottle, once a day, at around three weeks. She would not have any of it, though, and this proved to be a battle of wills as time went on. I had visions of picking up a screaming, hungry and dehydrated daughter from nursery each day, due to her stubborn refusal to drink her milk from a bottle. This proved to be a very stressful and difficult time, especially when the weeks started ticking by towards my return to work. I spent a small fortune on every type of teat and bottle on the market, and many hours crying my eyes out with Emily in my arms screaming and kicking in objection to the bottle. It was as though she thought I was cruelly teasing her, or even rejecting her, by not giving her the breast. I also became an expert at expressing milk for her, to see if it was the formula milk that she didn't like, as opposed to the actual bottle. The first time I tackled this task, it seemed as though I was at it all day for the measly reward of three ounces of breast milk. As I carefully tried to transfer the precious drops into a bottle, I somehow managed to spill the whole lot on the floor. I was so upset at my wasted efforts that I was sorely tempted to ignore all the sterilization rules just this once, mop the milk up with a dishcloth and wring it out into the bottle. I soon became an expert at this expressing business, though, and must have produced enough to feed a whole nursery. I still have ice-cube trays full of breast milk in my freezer, which I can't bring myself to throw away after all my hard work producing the stuff. I think the crunch will come when I unwittingly serve a guest their gin and tonic with two lumps of breast milk floating in it. Emily, however, had absolutely no respect for all the hours of humiliation and embarrassment I had put into suctioning my bosoms into this milking device, and still refused the bottle point-blank.

The whole breast-to-bottle experience was very traumatic and upsetting for both of us and I felt a tremendous amount of guilt, but, with the return-to-work clock ticking, I could not give in. After much perseverance, we eventually found an agreeable teat and an ideal milk temperature, and once Emily had given in to the bottle, she then decided her next trick would be to refuse to accept the bottle from anyone else but me. Great! There she was at the nursery with fully trained staff, and I had to go down every lunchtime to give her a bottle. I might as well have stuck to the breastfeeding!

I did still want to breastfeed at night on my return to work, but it was a very sad day a few weeks later when the weaning cycle was complete and Emily no longer wanted this one session. I not only lost the closeness of breastfeeding, but once my milk had dried up I soon lost my new-found B cup as well. Gavin didn't exactly make me feel better about this when he recently wound me up by saying, 'If you carry on shrinking at this rate you will soon be just a pair of nipples.'

Despite the difficult weaning period, two attacks of mastitis and two breast cysts, I have absolutely no regrets about breastfeeding. Emily did so well, she put on loads of weight and looked a complete picture of health to me, although others seemed to find her fuller figure hard to handle. Most people with new babies would get comments like, 'Ah, how sweet,' but all I ever heard was, 'Isn't she big?' or 'What a large baby!' and for some crazy reason these stupid comments got to me. I can remember Lime Lycra Lady bearing the brunt of my annoyance at a postnatal reunion, when she made what to me was yet another comment about Emily's size. It was the straw that broke the proverbial camel's back. 'Isn't she b –', she started to say, but before she could get any further I had retorted, '– a bonny, beautiful baby. Yes, you're quite right!', and then walked off before she had a chance to speak again.

I realize I was a little bit paranoid about Emily's size, but a friend recognized what I was going through and cheered me up by telling me that her daughter was over three and a half times her birth weight by the time she was four months old. Emily was only just over twice her birth weight at four months – positively sylph-like in comparison. I personally love to see a cuddly, happy, contented baby, and really don't understand why some people have a problem with that!

One of the most embarrassing incidents relating to breastfeeding was to do with breast pads. I started off using the Boot's-own brand, which were pink on one side and white on the other. I took Emily to meet my work colleagues on a hot summer afternoon, wearing an elegant sleeveless cream linen top that I was quite proud of being able to fit into. I couldn't understand why a few of my colleagues were looking rather strangely at my chest, until I went into the ladies' toilets, which were rather well lit, and looked in the mirror. Clear for all to see through my cream shirt were the embarrassing pink circular breast pads. It wasn't until we sat down to write this book and I shared this story with Lyndsey and Hilary that I learnt that I had been wearing the breast pads inside out! It really is frightening how the temporary brain shrinkage in pregnancy can cause such blatant stupidity. Well, I hope it is temporary, anyway. I would hate to think that I may be destined to make such a 'tit' of myself for the rest of my days!

Lyndsey

* * *

Before pregnancy I had the average 36B chest, which I had always been happy with since it was not too small and not too big, but I was soon concerned about the size it could grow to. In fact, it was my boobs that showed the first signs of pregnancy. They ached from dawn till dusk and back to dawn again and this persisted for several months. The aching was associated with a steady increase in size, moving from B cup to C cup, but fortunately that's where they stopped. Tim was overjoyed with this new shape and was disappointed to be told that they were off limits for the foreseeable future. It was whilst I was still coming to terms with my newly enlarged bustline that I overheard Tim on the phone. A concerned friend was ringing to find out how I was and Tim assured her that I was fine (apart from my early-morning close friendship with our toilet pan) and that signs of pregnancy were now evident – including my breasts, which now resembled bulbous onions. '*Bulbous onions!*' I proclaimed. 'Gee, thanks Tim – make me feel better, why don't you?' I bet Bruce Willis didn't describe Demi's boobs as bulbous onions before she paraded her body on the front covers of the glossies!

At thirty-nine weeks I bought my nursing bras, as I intended to breastfeed if I was able. I had been advised to buy those with the zipped cup – the zip could be left slightly undone on the side that you had just breastfed from, so that at the next feed, you would remember to use the other side. Also, they were supposed to be easier to reassemble than those that fastened at the bra strap, but I often wondered if this were true whilst trying to zip the cup back up, one-handed, sleeping babe in arms, the heavy, flabby boob getting caught in the zip – *ouch!* So much for the practicality of the zip-up – I was soon left with a line of blood blisters under each boob. When Tim heard I had bought these bras, you could see his eyes light up as if he were imagining a new sex toy with zips and black latex. So when he saw the twee white broderie anglaise, with all these blood blisters to boot, his fantasies took a nose dive.

One thing I will never forget about breastfeeding was the first time the midwife tried to get the baby latched on. Imagine the scene. I had just gone through twenty hours of labour. It was four o'clock in the morning and I had a midwife squeezing my boob between her thumb and forefinger as if her life depended on the measly drop of milk that she expected to obtain. Never mind the newborn, who didn't seem particularly keen to feed anyway and whose head she thrust on to my nipple like a crash-test dummy on an air bag. I felt like telling her to try squeezing her own boob like that and see how she liked it, but for some bizarre reason my brain and mouth had been disconnected and I just lay there and let the abuse continue. In fact, that humiliating ritual, whether carried out by midwife or health visitor, continued for a couple of weeks until they were convinced that Bethan was latching on properly. I began to dread the daily visits and I was glad when my boob was no longer being manipulated and forced into my baby's mouth by all and sundry. Once Bethan was latched on, I couldn't get over the pain that followed for the first twenty seconds or so until she was in full feeding mode. They certainly didn't prepare me for that experience, which had all my fingers and toes curled up and a facial expression that said it all, '*Good God* that hurt.' Having said how painful this latching-on process was, I must add that I think

I actually got off quite lightly. Bethan, it turned out, was positively gentle compared to other babies.

One lady I met at aerobics described the agony of feeding with cracked nipples. Just the description was enough to make my eyes water, and I believe that she has a permanent reminder of the pain in the form of two horrendous scars on her areolae – savage baby! Mind you, there was the time when Bethan was so hungry and frantic to start sucking that as I brushed my boob towards her, she lunged at it and suckered herself on to the flesh, rather than the nipple, and before I knew it I had a cracking love bite that even Dracula would have been proud of.

At about three weeks Bethan was feeding better, albeit at two-to-three-hourly intervals around the clock, and, relatively pain free, I was even able to start expressing milk so that Tim could do one of the night-time feeds. I thought that I had the hungriest baby ever, as the other girls said their babies were feeding every three to four hours. It was only later on that I discovered that while I had been timing the feeds from the end of one feed to the beginning of the next, the others were timing from the start of one feed to the start of the next. The recalculation to include the one-hour feeding time meant that Bethan was also feeding every three to four hours, so she wasn't the hungry little monster that I had previously thought.

Things appeared to be going well until around the three-week stage, when a lump appeared on my left breast, and I soon had mastitis. Two courses of antibiotics later it still hadn't cleared up, and I developed an abscess. As Bethan clocked up her seventh week, I was under general anaesthetic having the abscess drained. As the mastitis had progressed I'd had to stop feeding from the left breast, so Bethan was introduced to formula milk for every other feed, and then eventually for all feeds while I spent three days in hospital. Before things got to this stage, I had been advised to let Bethan feed from the infected breast as it might help clear it, but I decided against this when, as I massaged the lump, a globule of bright green pus oozed from my nipple. I had visions of this going into Bethan's stomach and her throwing up fluorescent sick, and scenes from *Alien* kept flashing into my mind. Although I was told that she would not be affected by it, I thought about how horrified I would have been if I knew my mother had made me suck out her infected pus in order to help clear an abscess, so I decided to draw the line at this. I must say that I was sad to stop breastfeeding because I enjoyed the closeness that it brought. I always knew it would have to stop at some stage, but I had not thought it would end so abruptly or under such horrible circumstances. In fact, I vividly remember our last breastfeed. It was four o'clock on the morning that I was due to go into hospital, and as I watched Bethan feed tears welled up in my eyes, as I knew I would never be able to have this closeness with her again. It was so lovely to have her soft face nestling into my breast – something a bottle just could not replace.

I had been told that they would cut in at the nipple to drain the abscess, which was about three inches above the nipple, and that there would be very little scarring. I was assured that it would be a quick overnight job followed up by some dressing changes. So when the dressing was removed for the first time, I was horrified to see a gaping wound about the size of a fifty-pence piece, stuffed with gauze dressing, right on top of my boob where the abscess had been. What happened to that small incision by the nipple, I asked myself? I was given morphine while the gauze was removed and the three-inch-deep hole repacked. God, I felt sick at the sight of it and wanted to die when they said this dressing would need to be changed daily for at least a month, a far cry from what I had expected. In fact I had follow-up care for five weeks, with a district nurse coming every day to change the dressing, which progressed from gauze to a seaweed-based dressing. I came to dread these visits even more than I'd dreaded the midwife's visits, and it is sad to say that my only encouragement was to see the dressing reduce from a full pack to half a pack and so on. Now I am left with a cracking scar that they say time will heal. So no more plunging necklines and Wonderbras for me. It's just as well I gave up any ideas of becoming a supermodel when I hit thirty!

Andrea

***

My boobs are the bane of my life, and they always have been. Most girls go through puberty gradually, but it seemed to happen overnight to me. It was sometime around my fourteenth birthday when my boobs popped up, like a pair of beach balls. It was as though the boob fairy had developed a wicked sense of humour and welded a pair of DD-cup boobs on to my thirty-four inch chest while I was sleeping, just for a bit of a laugh. I know that a lot of women would not complain, but I was always less than enamoured with them. They only got in the way of the tom-boyish sporting activities that took up most of my teenage years. Instead of wearing skimpy little numbers to show them off, I have always believed in the-baggier-the-better philosophy when it comes to clothing. You can imagine, then, my absolute horror when I recently discovered that my postnatal chest size had zoomed up to a hideous 38E, and even that is a little over-stretched! Realistically, I should possibly be an F cup, but as I have not plucked up the courage to ask for such a monstrosity, and as they do not appear to be readily available on the shelves, I have not yet progressed to the humungous-hammock look.

From the moment Max was born, I was desperate to get back to my sporting activities, but I had not anticipated quite how much my increased breast size was going to interfere. I had always been used to strapping them down, but suddenly absolutely nothing would tame them. For fear of two black eyes at my first game of football, I decided that drastic measures needed to be taken, and so I have worn two bras for all sporting activities. My team mates have changed the words of the song 'Three lions on my shirt' to 'Two bras on my chest'. All I can say is that it is a good job I am not breastfeeding, as poor Max would need to be Houdini to fight his way in through that lot! The one consolation I have for these excessive appendages is that I may yet score my lifelong dream goal. You know how footballers receive a ball in the air and control it on their chest? Well, in my dreams I receive a high ball and nestle it in my cleavage, thus enabling me to run the entire length of the pitch, ducking and diving my way through the opposition's defence, evading all of the tackles, skipping past the keeper and then simply tipping the ball out of my cleavage and into the net crying 'Look, no hands!' Now that should instantly earn me a place in the England ladies' squad!

Bruce, I must add, not only does not mind this part of my weight gain, but actively discourages me from doing any exercise which might reduce my boobs again. He has always been a man who likes his women top-heavy, so at least someone came out

Look, no hands!

happy! At one point I got so low about having to carry around these monstrosities that I took up a relative's suggestion to weigh them. This was an activity Bruce was happy to help with, as it involved me standing stark-naked on the scales while he took the strain off my boobs by holding them. It was more of a 'whey-hey' than a 'weigh' for him, but it made me feel stacks better when I discovered that I was carrying around over half a stone in my boobs alone!

Despite the size of my bust, breastfeeding was not something that proved to be successful for Max and me. We made a token effort at it in hospital, but Max was not very interested and I was not prepared for the ambush of midwives, who spent two hours at a time grappling with my boobs while a screaming Max did everything in his minute power to prevent my nipple going anywhere near his mouth. After giving birth, the last thing I wanted to go through was a battle of wills between a midwife and baby with my boob in the middle. At the point when the midwife told me I had funny-shaped nipples, I decided that I would just keep them to myself. I probably should have per-severed longer, and often think that I might have missed out on something by not breastfeeding, but when the midwife gave me a bottle for Max after the second failed attempt at the breast, he guzzled it so readily that I could not justify or endure a third battle of the boob. However, when I later asked a different midwife for a bottle for my baby, she looked at me as though I had asked her for a dose of arsenic to give the lad! With one look, she instantly managed to fill me with guilt and feelings of total failure. Luckily, Bruce was there at the time and took on a new-found protective role for his family by firmly telling the midwife, 'I don't think you understand – we are *not* breastfeeding. We would like a bottle.' This use of the royal 'We' did make me laugh, conjuring up the comical image of Bruce attempting to breastfeed – but it did the trick and bottles were provided from then on.

Two or three days later, my milk arrived. Unfortunately,

nobody had told my boobs that we were bottle-feeding, so I decided to have a second bash at breastfeeding. Max had other ideas, though – I think he thought I had totally lost my marbles when I shoved a boob in his mouth and told him it was his dinner. All I can say is that when he hits puberty I don't suppose he will turn his nose up so readily when he is offered a boob to suck on (but not mine, of course)!

Until my milk supply dried up, I was leaking like a constantly dripping tap. On the first night home, I got up to feed Max at three o'clock in the morning. Then afterwards, half asleep, I crawled back into my pit. As I snuggled down under my duvet I noticed a damp patch on the sheet. It was at the top end of the bed so I knew it was not a leak from down below. In my exhausted state, all intelligent logic went out of the window and the only plausible explanation I could come up with was a leaking pipe in the ceiling. Bruce thought he was having some kind of surreal dream when he woke up to find me, in the buff, up a stepladder by the bed, feeling the ceiling in a mad attempt to trace the leak. When I told him what I was doing, he brought me down to earth in his usual gentle and understanding way by saying, 'You silly cow – it's your *tits* leaking.' He has never been one to mince his words.

The big advantage of bottle-feeding was, of course, the fact that, right from day one, Bruce was able to do his fair share of the night shifts. I just wish that it had been his turn that night – it would have saved me waddling out to the garden shed at three in the morning, to fetch the stepladder, wearing nothing but my anorak and trainers. I am sure that this is not an activity that would have been recommended three days after giving birth, and quite what I thought I was going to do up the ladder once I had located the leaking pipe is way beyond me!

Hilary

***

My boobs started growing on a daily basis from the day I fell pregnant. I couldn't believe how fast they expanded. One day I was a 36B and before I knew it I was a DD! I thought my

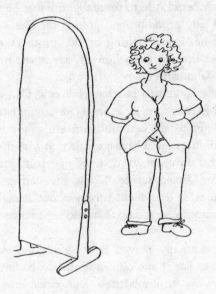

Time to invest in new bras, for certain

stomach would never overtake them. The world of DDs was a complete mystery to me. How come there are no BBs or CCs? Does DD mean bigger than D, or is it smaller, like AA is smaller than A? Intriguing as this was, I must admit I never enquired, so I am still none the wiser.

Being a complete cheapskate, though, I did not want to invest in new bras too often, so I kept squishing mine into my B-cup bras until, at twenty-five-weeks pregnant, I noticed that horrendous, tell-tale fatty syndrome of having what looks like four boobs! 'Time to invest in new bras, for certain,' I thought. I nipped into the local department store in my half-hour lunch break one day, and for the first time in my life, I braved asking advice from the bra-department women. Now, that was an experience! I am self-conscious enough at the best of times, but standing stripped to the waist in a changing room at twenty-five-weeks pregnant, with mirrors exposing my blubber from every angle, was a complete nightmare! Add to this delightful scene a very pleasant middle-aged lady prodding and poking me like a prize heifer, shaking her head and sighing at the prospect of my chest expanding yet further. I can honestly say it was nearly as big a nightmare as labour itself.

I eventually agreed to purchase my new DD-cup bra, and threw my shirt back on in a desperate attempt to regain my dignity and get to my afternoon meeting, for which I was already ten minutes late. I hasten to add that with the new-found knowledge that my chest was destined to expand yet further, and in the not-too-distant future, I only invested in the one bra and spent the next ten weeks rinsing it out at night and often wearing it damp the next day, as an added penance for my being tight-fisted.

When I eventually arrived at my afternoon meeting, now twenty minutes late, I apologized profusely, blaming a crisis on my patch at work for my lateness, and settled into the one free chair on the far side of the room in the circle of fifteen people. No sooner had I settled into the meeting than I looked down at my shirt, and with hot and cold horror realized that it was inside out! Yes, the size-sixteen label was dangling at the back of my neck for all to see. I had seams and cotton stitching right down my front with not a button in sight, and 'wash at forty degrees, do not dry clean' dangling at my right hip. At full sprint, I left the meeting within seconds of arriving, and on my return, fully and appropriately clothed, managed to blame morning sickness for my sudden absence and gained the sympathy of all! It is amazing how handy these symptoms of pregnancy can be. Even at twenty-five-weeks pregnant, no one questioned my extended suffering but merely gave me added sympathy.

Fortunately, my boobs had a rest from their growth spurt at the DD stage, giving my belly a chance to overtake. I waited with anticipation for them to start the leaking I had heard so much about, but it never came. My box of hundreds of breast pads sat waiting to come into their own, but my boobs never leaked, even after the birth. I think I must have extra strong valves on my nipples. I stuck the breast pads in my bra for the first week or two, but to be quite honest I think they had more use as drinks coasters when I forgot to put them back in after feeding Molly! I've got enough of them left over to wallpaper the lounge. I must be one of the only mothers who gained great satisfaction, and indeed pride, the first time her baby threw up, as it was the first sign I'd had that anything was actually coming out of my boobs. For all I knew before that, Molly could have been sucking fresh air!

And talking of sucking, my word, has Molly got a suck on her! She sucks like she's drinking a McDonald's thick shake through a very thin straw. My poor nipples, I reckon they have grown to at least twice their original size. I'm surprised that she doesn't gag on them! I'm telling you, forget 'chapel hat pegs' – mine are now full-blown coat rails!

Breastfeeding is something I went into very half-heartedly. I decided I would give it a go, but if the baby did not take to it straight away I was not going to get myself screwed up over it. I would go straight to the bottle. Well, I think Molly must have been listening from inside me, because she came out and took to it straight away, like a true professional! Ten minutes after she was born I was told to try breastfeeding. Now, there is a concept – one minute you're one person and the next you're not only a mother, but a breastfeeding mother! I hadn't a clue what I was doing and the midwives left us to it, so I just wopped out a boob from my nightie and roughly pointed Molly's head in the direction of it. She seemed to know exactly what to do and has never looked back.

Public feeding was my biggest fear. I kept looking at these maternity blouses with flaps to feed through. This was enough to put me off breastfeeding completely. The thought of slapping my boob out through a flap in my blouse was definitely beyond any of the mothering instincts I was meant to have – absolutely no way! It petrified me that something so private as my bust was now to be put on public display for all my friends and family to see. Being a very sociable and chatty person, to put it mildly, I was also not enamoured with the prospect of spending half of my life in a room on my own – well, with only a baby for company – just to ensure that I did not put my boobs on public display. Therefore I did not think that breastfeeding was going to be for me at all!

Well, I have managed to get around this problem by investing in some very baggy shirts and jumpers, and poor Molly has learnt to eat under wraps whenever we are in company. It's great. She goes completely underneath my clothes before I even release a boob, and lies there quite happily in privacy and darkness. The poor child will probably develop some kind of eating disorder when she is older, due to the deep psychological damage caused by me making her always hide to eat as a baby.

Molly is now three months old, and much to my amazement, I am still breastfeeding. I always said that if I was successful with this method of feeding I would stop at twelve weeks. I cannot stand seeing huge children, as opposed to babies, sucking on their mothers. Let's face it, if a child can actually undo your blouse to get to the food themselves, then they are likely to retain a memory of this method of feeding in their adult life. Now that really would cause psychological damage. If I had a memory of sucking on my mother's boobs, I think I would be sick at the very thought of drinking milk! Having said that, I cannot yet imagine how I am going to tackle weaning Molly off me. She is a determined little soul. I think that the moment of truth will come when she goes on to solids, because the thought of pureed carrot around my nipples, when she wants a drink after her meal, really does repulse me!

Sarah

* * *

My entry in this section pales into insignificance in comparison with my four mates. Being a modest 32B before pregnancy, I was looking forward to the inevitable expansion of my chest, and was delighted as my boobs grew to a grand 34B/C at the height of pregnancy. As boobs go, I realize that mine were still quite conservative, but it was a new-found pleasure for me to be able to display a cleavage for once in my life, without having to rely on a Wonderbra (or a 'sheep-dog bra' which David, Hilary's farmer husband, has reliably informed me 'rounds them up and brings them in!'). It was just a shame that my poor attempt at a Dolly Parton figure had to be accompanied by a large, bulging stomach.

During pregnancy, I had decided that I would have a good go at breastfeeding, as it seems to be the preferred method of nourishment for newborn babies, and after a while the midwives' 'breast is best' campaign does tend to rub off on you. The only drawback I could envisage was that, since for me my boobs are primarily sexual objects, I didn't know how I was going to take to having a baby permanently suckling from me. This same concern was voiced by Ms Textbook in our antenatal class. 'My breasts are for me and my husband,' she said. 'I have difficulty imagining feeding a baby from them.' My sentiments exactly, but something prevented me from openly agreeing with her when I suddenly had the horrific thought that my sex life might parallel hers in some textbook way!

My night in hospital after Jack was born was designed to give me a well-earned rest and also the opportunity to get as much expert tuition on breastfeeding as possible. I would probably have done just as well relying on Tim's assistance at home. I was woken at midnight by a bolshy midwife handing me Jack in the darkness of the postnatal ward and pronouncing, 'Your baby needs a feed.' As I struggled to come to from my semi-conscious, post-delivery traumatized state and sit up, she forcefully suggested that I feed Jack whilst lying down. What a nightmare! I had only managed to feed Jack twice before as it was, and that had been after several attempts, sitting in the customary upright position. Now there I was lying on my side, boobs peeking out from my buttoned-down maternity nightie, desperately contorting myself to offer first one nipple then the other, in the attempt to force-feed my brand-new baby. To make matters worse, Jack looked just as sleepy as I felt, and did not appear to want feeding at all. We eventually just cuddled up together and fell asleep. All I can say is that if that's a midwife's idea of a practical joke, it was in very bad taste. I was not in the mood for a laugh.

As it turned out, breastfeeding for me lasted six weeks in total. I was alternating breast and bottle-feeds by two weeks, and was rapidly won over by the ease and convenience of bottle-feeding. Jack was, and still is, a hungry baby, and needed more than I could supply. And as any good business student will tell you, when demand exceeds supply, you need to go find some more from elsewhere.

The experience of breastfeeding for me was pleasurable while it lasted. However, the hilarity of the side-effects and the accessories that go with it just have to be recorded. In the early days, I would wake up in the morning with Jack crying for food, run to the loo to empty my bladder before feeding him, and find to my horror that the front of my nightdress was totally soaked. Leaning over the sink to wash my face, I had the impression that there were three taps running simultaneously. It was a strange sensation seeing my nipples, which were for me, as already mentioned, first and foremost a sexual part of my body, dripping involuntarily with milk. I never did work out whether it was Jack's cries that triggered my milk supply or whether it was purely an overload which needed to be emptied in some way. Whatever it was, it necessitated me wearing my two maternity nightdresses on alternate nights to save the bed from an Andrea experience. I would cringe as I imagined the neighbours commenting, 'She's got that same nightie on the line *again*. She's either got a fetish about purple and white striped maternity night-wear or she's obsessed with cleanliness. Poor love, it must be her hormones.'

On the third day after Jack was born, my boobs became severely engorged, particularly the left one, which he then had trouble latching on to. I just continued feeding him on the right side in the vain hope that the left side would go down of its own accord, but of course it didn't. I can still see him now, rooting around for the nipple, his tiny face bouncing off my engorged boob like a bouncing bomb on a lake, and getting more and more frustrated at the lack of forthcoming food. On the recommendation of the visiting midwife I sent Tim down to the local supermarket to buy some cabbage to alleviate the discomfort of my bursting breast. Cabbage apparently contains enzymes which, when a leaf is fitted neatly inside your bra against the offending boob, soothes the taut skin and calms the stinging sensation. A few minutes later, Tim returned gallantly proffering a bag of shredded cabbage. He looked quite hurt when I turned him straight round and sent him running back to buy a whole cabbage with *leaves*. When he returned at last with a nice green summer cabbage, he smartly had the last word. 'I asked the lady for a B-cup cabbage, so I hope it fits!'

Having initially been revolted by the idea of stuffing cabbage leaves into my maternity bras, it has to be said that the cabbage treatment worked wonders. For three days I paraded Jack around family and friends quite oblivious to the distinctive aroma that followed in my wake. This smell of rotting cabbage wafting up my collar was a small price to pay for soothed boobs!

Fortunately, I didn't breastfeed long enough to need a breast pump. I know that lots of women get on marvellously with them, but for me they have an uncanny resemblance to those large industrial milking machines you see on farmyard documentaries. However, I remember the occasion when, at a postnatal reunion organized by the health visitors, I was approached by a girl offering me her breast pump – free of charge! The reason for her generous offer was that she herself 'had so much milk she didn't know what to do with it all'. I politely turned her down and left the reunion utterly puzzled. Was she actually trying to donate her breast milk to me (I was sure Jack didn't look that under-nourished) or had she merely misunderstood the reason for a breast pump? I fear it was the latter (poor thing!) – a breast pump is exactly what she needed to drain off her excess milk and not, as she may have thought, to get the flow going in the first place. The shrunken brain obviously affects us all in different ways.

On the subject of breast pumps, Tim, Jack and I went to the wedding of a close friend when Jack was two weeks old, and I took with us a supply of bottles, already prepared, and unre-servedly fed Jack as and when he demanded. It was during one of these feeds that a woman came up to me and exclaimed in a rather disparaging tone, '*Only* two weeks old and you are *bottle-feeding!*'. I later found out that she had spent the whole of the previous week attached to a breast pump in order to be able to express enough milk to leave her two-month-old daughter with a friend for the day, so that she could attend the wedding. It obvi-ously takes a braver woman than me to handle such apparatus.

I am sad to report that I'm convinced that my chest size has reduced to less than it was before my pregnancy. In fact, I'm so convinced that I really do not have the courage to go back to John Lewis to be measured for a post-pregnancy bra. I don't think my pride would let me go through anything as embarrassing as being escorted into the pubescent girls' bra department, away from the lacy underwired numbers that require a tad more than a bee sting to fill them. It will no doubt mean that my sheep-dog bras are really going to come into their own, helped along by two hundred press-ups a day to ensure that I keep those muscles well toned.

The Battle of the Bulge

It is difficult to say which subject, boobs or weight gain, takes the greater emphasis in pregnancy, but I think that weight gain just tips the scales!

At the beginning you find yourself fixated on pregnant women, estimating how many weeks 'gone' they are, and asking yourself questions like 'Will I be that big then, when I am that many weeks?' 'Has she put on weight anywhere other than the bump?' and 'Does her belly button stick outwards yet?' There are so many intriguing elements to this unbelievable concept of your stomach swelling up to such giant proportions in such a short space of time. How does the skin stretch so far and what the hell happens to it afterwards? The image of being able to roll up your stomach and tuck it into either your bra or trousers was certainly one to be avoided. These drastic changes to your body occur so quickly that none of us had any problem putting together our tales about this area.

Some of us were lucky enough to sail through pregnancy without expanding too much, while others came out looking like your average-sized adult African elephant! Some of us flaunted our bellies, while others would have worn hessian sacks if they had been guaranteed to conceal the bulge. Some of us stretched and stretched without a single mark, while others marked and marked without much stretch at all!

But, despite the amazingly different tales we all had to tell, in our final months we each had seats given up for us on public transport by anyone and everyone (even if some of us fitted into them better than others), and we were generally spoilt rotten, which was marvellous. One of our lasting memories was that this was the only time in our lives when the fatter we got, the more respect we seemed to be shown, or perhaps it was just sympathy! Either way, it was definitely a bonus.

Lyndsey

* * *

For me, this will be a brief section as I was fortunate not to put on too much weight, but I have to admit that not having scales did help to evade the issue. However, having said this, it wasn't a promising beginning, because my stomach and waistline soon expanded and by three months anything without an elastic or stretch waistband was impossible to wear. Fortunately, things settled down then and any increase in my weight after that was associated with the increase in my bump, and I was quite pleased when people commented, 'You are all baby.' Apparently, from behind you would never have known I was pregnant. There was one occasion, however, when I did not feel so sylph-like, and that was when I attended my friend's wedding when I was thirty-four weeks pregnant. I could have killed her. She had waited all these years to tie the knot, and now had to do it when I resembled a barrage balloon. I pleaded with her to change the date from May to September but she was not to be persuaded, so my next nightmare was, what on earth was I going to wear? After scouring the shops and catalogues, I did manage to find the proverbial tent to cover the bump, but I would hardly have called my outfit elegant. You can picture it now – the usual photo of friends was called for and as the lens panned the line-up, there were my slim-line size-ten mates in their slinky new outfits with show-stopping hats. Then poking out from behind, as I refused to be in the front line, was the now chubby blonde with the big bump. I've always felt like an Amazon woman compared to the rest of the petite line-up, so the additional bulk didn't help the issue. Needless to say, I shall not be displaying the photos and I'll probably insist that my friend burns all the negatives!

Hilary had a giggle at my expense when we went shopping when I was thirty-nine weeks pregnant and she was thirty-seven weeks. I was flagging and, before we left, Hilary needed to pop into Marks and Spencer for some last-minute buys, so I said I would sit outside and wait. I had spied a space, between two older men, on a bench outside the store. I reversed up to it, asked the gents if there was room for a little one and promptly planted myself between them. I have never been great at ten-pin bowling, but I reckon on that occasion I nearly got a 'strike' as I rolled into the space and just about knocked the two old boys off either end of the bench. Hilary just about gave birth with laughter as she ambled off to do her shopping, bemused that I was living under the illusion that I was still a size ten.

Another thing which I failed to acknowledge had gone during my pregnancy was the ability to park my car in *any* space, no matter how tight a fit it was. Basically, as long as the gap between two cars was wide enough for me to fit my head out when I opened my door, I had previously been able to get in and out. The number of times I parked in such spaces when I was pregnant I would hate to guess at. I would open my door to discover a

On a mission to find a fat ladies' parking space

gap just about big enough to fit a cigarette paper through. Unperturbed by this, I would attempt to back my way out of my car, nursing my bump as I went in order to avoid injury from protruding handles and door mechanisms. If I did successfully negotiate my way out of the car, the next battle was getting past that narrow point where the two cars' wing-mirrors protrude simultaneously, leaving no gap at all. The options at this point were either to mountaineer over the bonnet or limbo underneath, so often it ended with me nursing my bump back through the minuscule gap and into the driver's seat, and defeatedly leaving on a mission to find a fat ladies' parking space. Never mind 'baby on board' car stickers – I think someone should invent a 'fat lady – please do not park too close to the driver's door' car sticker, because this really is an essential requirement during pregnancy.

All in all, I think I gained about two stone, but judging by the Niagara Falls that flowed when my waters broke, I believe I was carrying at least a stone of water. I then lost the remainder in the first couple of weeks after the birth, largely due to breastfeeding but also because I was so stressed out. I seemed to spend all the hours of the day and night either feeding or nursing the baby, which meant that I never found a minute to grab a bite to eat. With hindsight, I should have been drinking plenty of milk at least, but not being a big milk drinker, even that did not occur to me. Tim was excellent in terms of ensuring that I had plenty to eat once the midwife had explained to him that I needed feeding up. As he watched me lose weight before his very eyes, he decided that enough was enough – he had to remedy the situation for fear that he would come home one evening to find his baby daughter in the arms of a skeleton wearing a zip-up maternity bra. I was left appetizing lunches and had gourmet meals cooked for me in the evenings. It was great! I remember one morning Tim had got up to do the five o'clock feed, leaving me to doze off back to sleep. Before I knew it, it was seven-thirty and Tim was waking me with a peck on the cheek, a mug of hot fresh coffee, and a warm, buttery croissant. He informed me that he had made a shepherd's pie for dinner, which I was instructed to place in the oven at six-thirty. What a star!

My weight deteriorated further in the two weeks following my operation to remove the breast abscess. This decline actually left me weighing less than I had pre-pregnancy, but fortunately soon took an upturn and now, three months later, I am back to my pre-pregnancy weight and fighting to keep it this way. As for stretch marks, I can't comment. I was lucky enough to escape these. However, there will always be my two-inch scar across my left breast as a subtle reminder of Bethan's first few weeks in the world.

Sarah

* * *

I also got off quite lightly on the weight-gain front. Jack is now four months old and I'm fighting the flab on my bum and thighs, which are my usual stubborn areas, but in total I only put on ten kilos (or twenty-two pounds, if you still think in imperial). I am now back to sixty-one kilos – only two more kilos to lose.

Having always been one of those sickening people who can proudly boast of a naturally flat and well-toned stomach, I have been dismayed to realize how long it takes to restore it to its pre-pregnancy state. While attending the antenatal exercise classes, I was horror-struck by the story of an exercise freak who allegedly continued doing rigorous sit-ups during her pregnancy and afterwards had the most horrendous gap between her stomach muscles, which were never to knit together again. I took heed from the tale and was extremely careful not to overdo it.

One of the big things that struck me in pregnancy was how my body was no longer my own, and I don't mean that it was my baby's either! I was groped and prodded more times in these nine months than in the whole of the rest of my life put together.

From the day I announced my pregnancy, everyone seemed to think that they had free rein to touch my stomach, at any available opportunity, without giving me any prior warning. Even in the early weeks, colleagues would just lean over for a quick touch. This sudden invasion of my body not only left me with no time to suck everything into its correct position before impact but also, in the early months when the baby was no bigger than a big toe, it meant that the people were really affectionately stroking what amounted to my lunch and my rapidly reducing muscle tone.

On the recommendation of a good friend, I touched my stomach immediately after Jack was born and, true to her prediction, it felt like blancmange – a massive blancmange of utterly shot muscle. However, the grossness of it didn't really hit me until after I got home from hospital and found that I still looked about six months pregnant – my maternity wear was still essential and was not to be immediately boxed away in the attic, as I had hoped. I had genuinely, but naïvely, expected my originally nice firm stomach to pop back into shape straight after the birth, but it didn't. After all, when your stomach muscles have just spent the past nine months stretching to breaking point, it is hardly surprising that they don't ping back to their original size like an elastic band – more's the pity! A couple of friends who visited me two days after Jack was born found it particularly amusing to witness the midwife's brief inspection of my tummy because, as I laughed at the feel of her cold hands, my middle wobbled, literally wobblbblbbbled, all over the place. If nothing else, it was a great source of entertainment for my friends, who were chuffed to see Sarah with a flabby stomach.

What I wasn't prepared for was the amount of exercise required to get the stomach, bum and thighs back into shape after having a baby. I'm now four months post-delivery and counting. I can't wait for that gross rubbing of the inner thighs to stop, and to be able to enjoy wearing tight jeans with confidence once again. It really is rather sad how ecstatic I became when, after spending the best part of ten minutes squeezing my legs and bum into my favourite pair of formerly loose-fitting trousers, I finally managed to do up the zip. The fact that I could do nothing for the rest of the day except stand bolt upright, with a wicked grimace on my face, was irrelevant – an important step had been made and, despite the massive discomfort, I was very proud of myself. Unfortunately, after all my efforts, I still had to wear my upper clothing very much untucked. This was not just because it was quite impossible to fit even the thinnest blouse material into my waistband along with my blancmange, but also because of that nightmare lippy look you get around the crotch when trousers are a tad tight. It was borderline pornographic and definitely not for public viewing! These wardrobe-reunion milestones seem almost as momentous as your baby's first smile and first tooth, and they spur you on to the next aerobics session and away from the temptation of cream cakes. Needless to say, I think I had better leave aspirations about getting back into my mini-skirts until volume two!

As for stretch marks, I came off very lightly in this area, too. So far, I can count one on my right hip. I did religiously rub various oils, lotions and creams into my bump and thighs every night, but whether that had any preventative effect, I don't know. I also drank raspberry-leaf tea by the gallon from thirty-five weeks onwards. I know it's supposed to help strengthen your uterus and make your contractions more effective during labour, but maybe it also has an as yet undetected stretch-mark-prevention effect as well. There are so many old wives' tales about stretch marks and how to prevent them – rub in this, bathe in that, eat this, don't eat the other. You can believe a whole lot of twaddle if it makes you feel better but, at the end of the day, I think a lot of it is hereditary.

Hilary

* * *

Weight gain was something I was always quite fearful of, as I had struggled to maintain my weight at nine and a half stone for years by means of exercise and a healthy diet, and I knew from previous experience that if I ever cut down on the exercise or increased my food intake the weight piled on. It is as though every morsel I eat goes straight in my mouth and down to my thighs and bum. I reckon if they cut open my thighs they would actually find the telltale evidence of chocolate bars and slices of cake fully intact sitting in there. Unfortunately, I had to cut out exercise very early on in my pregnancy due to a scare when it was thought I was losing my baby, and I did not resume any real exercise until I was past the twenty-four-week survival zone. By then it was far too late – my bum and boobs were protruding equally far but in opposite directions, which meant that when I turned sideways I looked like the letter S!

Because of a previous obsession with my stomach muscles (I did a hundred and fifty sit-ups every morning pre-pregnancy), it took my stomach a hell of a long time to look pregnant. Throughout my pregnancy, I used to get David to stand parallel with the bathroom door, then I would inch my way out naked and get him to say what came out first, my belly or my boobs! I felt so self-conscious of my 'blub' that I wanted to wear an 'I'm not fat, I'm pregnant' badge, but unfortunately the fact that I was now both fat and pregnant would have been a far more realistic statement to broadcast, though not nearly as appealing!

A four-weekly ritual started when I was twenty weeks. I got myself into my swimming costume and made David take a photo of my side view, in the way I had seen it done in magazines, to show the progression of pregnancy. I thought it would be a nice bit of memorabilia. However, unlike the sylph-like stunners whom the magazines managed to find for their monitoring, my pictures demonstrated the type of pregnancy they somehow fail to mention. With progressive water retention, my ankles bore a remarkable resemblance to tree trunks, and my expanding stretch marks and chronic cellulite made me look more like a 'before' advert for plastic surgery than an advert for healthy pregnancy.

Water retention started at about twenty-eight weeks, when I realized I could not get my rings off. This was not a major hassle, but when my feet and ankles expanded by two sizes I was really gutted. The only shoes I could fit into were my flip flops, which did not create a great impression at work. It is very difficult to get the psychiatric consultant to take you seriously in a meeting when you look dressed for the beach.

Stretch marks started to appear on my bum at twenty-nine weeks, and having never seen them before I couldn't believe my eyes when I first got them. I had got out of the bath, and as I bent down to dry my legs I caught a glimpse of my backside in the mirror. It looked as though I had been savaged by a wild beast, leaving enormous red claw marks streaking across each cheek. David initially thought I had been sitting on a rough surface and that the marks would fade, but when they were still shining brightly the next morning we realized they were definitely there to stay. I consoled myself that they were only on my bum, and nobody except David would ever see them – and since it was his fault that I had them anyway, he had no right to complain! I am not sure whether it was naïvety or wishful thinking that made me believe they would not spread any further, but whichever it was, I was definitely wrong, and ended up with the beast paying further visits to my thighs, waist and lower stomach. At one of the antenatal classes, a lady visited with her baby to offer some calming words to us, the prospective mothers. I don't know about calming, but when she started breastfeeding during her talk and I saw the enormous stretch marks down her boob, I was almost apoplectic! It was one thing having the whole lower half of my body looking like it had had a close encounter with a scarlet lipstick, but to have my boobs completely wrecked too petrified me. Fortunately, to date they have escaped this peril. Mind you, I will not speak too soon, because with the constant expansion and reduction as they fill and empty each day with milk, there is still time! I have to agree with Sarah, though, when she says that all the theories about creams to stop stretch marks are a load of codswallop. I splashed every lotion and potion imaginable all over my body, to no avail. However, I think she is being extremely diplomatic citing hereditary factors as the probable cause. Forget hereditary factors – I think what she really meant was hefty and fat! At the end of the day, Andrea and I were the ones who piled on the weight and also piled on the stretch marks. The other three with their perfect bonny bumps and no bums did not have a single scar in sight. So I reckon the moral of the story has got to be that if you don't want stretch marks, don't let your skin stretch in the first place.

Now Molly is born, I still have two stone to lose before getting back to a weight I will tolerate. The pounds are hardly falling off, but then dieting and breastfeeding are not exactly compatible. So there is not a great deal I can do – yet! Well, that is my excuse and I'm sticking to it. I have set myself some targets and will not buy myself any new clothes until I have lost all the weight. This is not too difficult a sacrifice, since at the moment I can't say that prancing around in a communal changing room is very appealing at all.

Underwear, however, is a different story altogether! I have not bought any new undies since before I was pregnant, which means that my current knickers look as though they have been through a war. They have expanded to accommodate my bulge, leaving the elastic completely shot, and without going into too much detail, maternity sanitary towels do not entirely meet the demands of their job! My underwear is now a complete embarrassment, never to be seen by anyone. I will not even peg it on the line to dry for fear that it may be viewed, and we live on a farm in the middle of nowhere. The only passers-by are sheep and I don't really think they would be too perturbed by the state of my pants!

The one thing I did purchase was a pair of those knickers designed to hold everything in at the front, but what a nightmare these proved to be. It is a bit like squeezing a tube of toothpaste – at the end of the day, it has got to come out somewhere. So as fast as your stomach is squashed in, the blub is bulging out either over the top, creating a spare tyre around the waist, or out of the leg holes, creating chronic 'visible panty line' and a squidge of fat on each inner thigh. *Most* attractive!

As with most women, this is a subject I could chomp on about all day. I am waiting now to find out if the weight will all just fall off when I stop breastfeeding. Some people say it falls off if you breastfeed, but as that has not happened I am going with the second theory, which is that fat is stored more readily while you are breastfeeding in order to provide spare food for the baby, but once you stop feeding it all just drops off. That sounds great to me. It is amazing how you can adapt the theories to make you feel better!

Andrea

* * *

After the initial excitement when I first discovered I was pregnant, I decided that I would have to change my eating habits. I had always been able to keep my weight at an acceptable level due to all the sport I did, so I just used to eat whatever I wanted, whenever I fancied it. I knew that this would have to change during my nine pregnant months, otherwise I would just turn into one of the little fat Greek ladies I mentioned earlier, but thirty years too soon. So I set myself lots of new healthy-eating guidelines – cutting out chocolate, chips and junk food and eating plenty of fruit and vegetables instead.

This new regime lasted around one week, until at about the seven-week stage I was hit by the dreaded morning sickness. I am extremely proud of the fact that during this nightmare period, which lasted six weeks, I did not go sick from work. I think the colleagues I was working with at the time wished I had, though, because I was a real misery on the morning shifts, and it cannot have been too pleasant for them when I had to stop the car every five minutes to throw up in the gutter. I soon realized that I could only bear to eat food that was extremely fattening and bad for me. Firstly, where most people had a biscuit in the morning before they got up, I would keep a whole packet of Ginger Nuts by the side of the bed and eat at least six with a cup of tea before risking a trip to the bathroom. I would then eat a bowl of cereal, one of the sugary rather than branny varieties, and leave for work. I would be sick on arrival at work without fail, and then after wasting my morning intake, would have to indulge in a mid-morning snack of a bacon and cheese puff, followed by a cake. Lunch would invariably involve a portion of chips, more cake and a can of fizzy drink, with an afternoon snack of a KitKat just to keep me going. Naturally, when I got home I would be starving, so I would need another bowl of cereal to tide me over till dinner. Generally this would be a nice fattening takeaway, because cooking made me feel sick. Well, that realistically describes my eating habits in the early stages of pregnancy. Oh, did I mention a bowl of cereal before I went to bed? I don't actually know how I survived without any food through the night, but then again I always had the Ginger Nuts on the bedside table in case of a midnight crisis!

Unfortunately, my morning sickness also reared its ugly head in the form of travel sickness, and boy did we have some fun with this. The usual ritual on any journey longer than ten minutes was for me to scream '*Now*' at the crucial moment. Bruce would then perform a textbook emergency stop and I would open the door and puke in the gutter without even needing to get out. On a certain trip to Highbury, the Arsenal ground, we were driving down Holloway Road when it suddenly came on. It was a very busy Saturday near Christmas and I just could not perform the gutter routine in front of all the shoppers. For fear of the effect on his upholstery, Bruce's improvisation skills came into play. He hunted the car for something suitable, but all he could find was a tube of tennis balls. Within seconds tennis balls were flying through the air and I was getting very intimate with the empty tube. It is amazing how good a seal there is on a tube that's not designed for holding liquid! Bruce, however, was not quite so confident in me or the tube, and spent most of the journey sympathizing but saying, 'Don't you *dare* spill any!' The consoling thing was that I always felt great just after I had been sick, so I was still able to enjoy my chicken sandwich and chips at the ground. Incidentally, Arsenal won three–nil – Max's first game, from the inside!

By the time the morning sickness had subsided, I had put on so much weight and was enjoying eating all of my favourite fattening foods so much that I did not see the point of stopping. I decided I would just have to diet afterwards and do extra exercise. At least I can say that I did eat well during my pregnancy, in fact I ate for England! Unlike the Bonny Bump Gang, who I really don't believe can possibly have eaten anything at all during the entirety of theirs.

When I went on maternity leave, I really went to town with the lunches out with Annette. I think she probably wishes she had not met me, because she was a candidate for the Bonny Bump Gang until I introduced her to all-you-can-eat pizza deals and various pub lunches. Being a good friend, I would always make sure that she had a very fattening chocolate dessert as well, just to make me feel better.

Having described my excessive eating habits, it will come as no surprise to learn that I suffered very badly with stretch marks. I cannot remember exactly at what stage they first appeared, but it was all quite amusing. I assumed that stretch marks came on your tummy, because that is where the skin stretches the most, so when I noticed a strange rash on the bum one morning I was a bit concerned. I had read in a book about a rare liver condition in pregnancy, the only symptom of which was a rash, so with my pregnancy paranoia I rushed off to the surgery for an examination. The doctor ummed and aahed and decided to take a blood test to check that my liver was functioning properly. I panicked for the next few days until the result came through giving me the all-clear. A day or two later, I had to laugh when I saw that the rash had developed into stretch marks which went from my thighs up my bum and on to my hips. Bruce immediately announced that I looked like a road map of Europe. I must be one of the only people who had to endure a blood test for a diagnosis of stretch marks. From that day on, the stretch marks just kept coming until basically I was covered in them from just above my knees to just below my chest. Never mind worrying about wearing a bikini in future, I couldn't even see myself wearing shorts again! So when Annette said one day at the swimming pool, 'I think I've got a stretch mark,' you can understand why I wasn't too sympathetic. Just having few enough to be able to count them would have been heaven to me!

Lyndsey sickened me with her reference to the fact that she did not look pregnant from behind. I would love to be able to say that I suffered from the same problem, but the reality is that I required a police escort for carrying a wide load when I went out and about. I cannot mention exactly how much weight I put on, partly because I just did not weigh myself at all for fear of what I would find, and partly because I would not want to scare anyone. All I can say is, forget talking in pounds or kilos as Sarah did – I am talking in stones, and enough of them to set up a beach to match Brighton! I will admit that I did weigh myself once when I was very heavily pregnant and discovered that I weighed more than Bruce, and he is no Charles Atlas. That really hit me and I knew that I would have to work very hard to get back in shape. In my defence, I have now been on a diet for a while, and slowly but surely I am getting there. I tried on my uniform the other day and it fitted, although admittedly not quite as comfortably as it used to. If I made no attempt to sit down or

than me – well, she needed more biscuits anyway! So everything was going quite smoothly until I met Andrea through the ante-natal classes, and it then went rapidly downhill. Instead of fruit, vegetables and fish, it was more a case of fudge, very tasty chocolate puddings and fish and chips. I like to hold Andrea totally responsible for my downfall, and have not let her forget it! When the antenatal classes began, Andrea and I would meet up and indulge in a frivolous lunch beforehand, to give us the strength for the afternoon's exercises. It was very enjoyable, but generally involved at least three courses, which weren't exactly essential at lunchtime. Don't get me wrong, I am delighted to have met Andrea, and we spent lots of time together sharing our fears and concerns about the pending births, and we have become great friends. I just did not want to share her weight gain too! Maybe if I had met her a little later in my pregnancy I might have been able to hold back on the hog-outs by a few months and not piled on the pounds so rapidly. Once the weight had started to mount up, though, I developed that dreaded comfort-eating syndrome of 'I'm fat anyway so a few treats won't hurt.'

Another side-effect of the ever-expanding bump was the dreaded protruding belly button. It first reared its ugly head at around the twenty-five-week stage, and although this provided me with the opportunity to give it a really good clean while it was inside out, it greatly limited my wardrobe. Unfortunately, I was at the height of pregnancy in the summer months, which meant that no matter what I wore, there it was sticking out through the material like a third nipple on a very cold day! I hated it, and tried absolutely everything to conceal it. I feigned being cold-blooded for as long as possible and continued to wear jumpers, but when the temperature hit the eighties I had to give in to flimsy, more revealing attire, and even resorted to Elastoplast in a desperate bid to strap it down. There was no holding back this one-eyed belly monster though, and within an hour it had fought its way past the plaster and was proudly greeting everyone in its full glory again. The thing that really amazed me, though, was that after Emily was born it didn't pop straight back in. I mean, it's one thing having a protruding belly button when you are pregnant, but walking around postnatally with Cyclops' friend in front of me was a complete embarrassment.

Unfortunately, unlike the rest of the girlies, I had to return to work quite soon after Emily's birth. This not only meant I was no longer able to attend the twice-weekly postnatal aerobics, but also that I had to buy an entire new work wardrobe. After just three months there was no way I was going to fit into my old suits, and maternity wear was a definite no-no. Having now invested in some larger clothing, I am no longer in such a hurry to lose the added weight – after all, I want to get my money's worth out of my new suits! That's the excuse I'm currently using to maintain my enjoyment of food for just a bit longer before I have to give in and start the hard and boring slog of dieting again. I would have liked to profess to being on a strict diet already, but Andrea would know it was a blatant lie. When she recently visited, I popped to the toilet, leaving her in my kitchen. I had briefly forgotten about her obsession with food and came back to find her drooling over all the scrummy fattening goodies in my larder. I have promised to invest in a padlock before she next comes to babysit to help her avoid the temptation, but I still have an image of her arriving tooled up with a crow-bar, just in case the munchies get the better of her while I'm out.

Stretch marks were something I was determined not to get, and so I decided to invest as much money as necessary to avoid them occurring. I bought various potions containing lanolin, AHAs and Vitamin E, and I naïvely thought that they were working until a colleague suggested that I perform the mirror test. So at thirty-four weeks I took a hand mirror and used it to look at the underside of my bump. And, too true, there the red devils were, wriggling their way up from my knicker line. Once they had been spotted, they seemed to go through a growth spurt, and before I knew what was going on, my tummy looked like a red-veined version of Stilton cheese. At the time I was horrified, but I realize now that compared to Andrea and Hilary I was very fortunate to get them only on my bump. They have now shrunk back down into the pubic area and are hardly visible at all, so I do believe I will be able to wear a bikini with confidence next summer – as long as I can shed my spare tyre by then, anyway.

I had secretly hoped that the theory about weight falling off after breastfeeding was finished was true. But much as I hate to disillusion Hilary, it hasn't happened. I stopped feeding Emily nearly a month ago now, and I think it's time I faced the reality that the only way to shed the weight will be through diet and exercise – shame!

I Must, I Must Improve My Bust, Belly, Buttocks . . .

Exercise in pregnancy is something most women tend either to step up a level or sit out completely. In most pregnancy books, there are lovely photographs of healthy, smiling women with beautiful big bellies striding out through parks, riding bikes or sitting in the lotus position in their pretty pastel-coloured tracksuits. What we were not prepared for were the fears and emotions that come with pregnancy which somewhat hinder this picture of an idyllic life. The early feelings of complete exhaustion and nausea are not exactly conducive to the urge to exercise. The fear of losing the baby initially puts paid to any strenuous exercise, and once this fear is over, the simple fact that no matter how much you exercise you are still getting bigger and bigger does very little for motivation! Most people exercise as a means to an end – better stomach-muscle tone, thinner thighs, smaller backside, and so on. So when your body keeps getting larger and larger despite all your efforts, forget the smiling pretty pastel-pink-tracksuit image, you need nothing short of a bomb under your bum to make sure you maintain a minimal level of fitness. Well, we have been lucky enough to have each other to act as our metaphorical bombs, both ante- and postnatally. So, as a result, we are all proud to say that we each have something to contribute to this chapter and there is not a couch potato amongst us, although admittedly we have all had our moments.

Lyndsey

* * *

Exercise is something that we are told to continue while pregnant, and my incentive was based on the misguided belief that if I maintained a basic level of fitness it would lead to an easier labour. Boy, how wrong I was. Or was it the level of exercise I chose that let me down?

Before pregnancy, I managed to drag myself along to one or two aerobic sessions a week, but it was always with a heavy heart and, to be honest, it was mostly a guilt trip because Tim is such a fitness freak. The constant jibes and occasional poke in the flabby stomach were enough to send me to the gym!

During the first couple of months of pregnancy, I felt so tired by the end of each day that I couldn't face the thought of a high-impact aerobic session, so I opted for the sofa, the TV and a cup of hot chocolate. However, the guilt trip was still there, and of course there were always Tim's endearing words, 'I don't want to be married to a bloater after this baby is born.' So when the midwife at the antenatal classes promoted the Saturday morning antenatal exercise class at the local sports centre, I decided to attend. What I didn't bargain for was the free swim that followed these classes. The social aspect of the class was definitely an essential factor in my continued attendance, and it became my lifeline to other relatively sane mums-to-be, namely Sarah and Hilary, who were on the same wavelength as me. There was, of course, one oddball, who became known to us as the Barmy Bank Manager. It never ceases to amaze me how people with so little common sense can reach such prestigious positions in the workplace. I'll explain further. Now you don't have to be a genius to take an educated guess as to where the pelvic-floor muscles are located, whether or not you are familiar with the Rocky Horror pelvic thrust. The fact that they are constantly mentioned by the health professionals as essential muscles to exercise in preparation for childbirth must surely indicate to all women the precise location of this muscle group. However, our Barmy Bank Manager didn't seem to have a clue. How do I know this? Well, it became apparent when the aerobic instructor, having given a lengthy explanation as to why it is so important to exercise the pelvic-floor muscles, then instructed us to stand, knees slightly bent, and pull these muscles 'Up, up, down, down.' As there is nothing to see when doing this exercise, the instructor cupped her hands in front of her and lifted them 'Up, up, down, down,' whilst we squeezed and relaxed our insides. It was then, out of the corner of my eye, that I noticed the Barmy Bank Manager, and yes, you've guessed it, there she stood, knees bent, hands cupped, lifting them 'Up, up, down, down' just like the instructor. How on earth she thought that this gentle hand action was going to help her maintain bladder control postnatally is beyond me. I wondered how she coped as a bank manager, if she could not even grasp this basic concept. I could imagine going to her for advice on investing an inheritance and coming out with a bank loan!

Although I enjoyed the exercise class, the dreaded swim was always there to haunt me, but as the other girls seemed so enthusiastic I dutifully went along with them. They would argue that to say I went *swimming* was an exaggeration. It was more of a pootle up and down the pool, with most of the time spent at either end having a chat. My swimming did improve, however, when the Barmy Bank Manager, who suffered from verbal diarrhoea, was swimming towards me with her mouth at full throttle – that was enough to get anyone swimming like Duncan Goodhew. In fact, I should be thankful to her for all those extra lengths that I did. I didn't realize just how many extra until the week when she didn't come for the swim. I did my usual routine of swim, chat, swim, chat, chat, swim, etc., and thought I had done rather well until I left the pool and the lifeguard stopped me to say, 'I don't know why you don't stay at home and have

a bath for the amount of exercise you get here!' What he failed
to realize was that I needed the volume of water that the swimming pool offered to support my ever-increasing weight. My
bath was quite simply no longer up to the job; he should just
have been grateful I didn't take a bar of soap in with me too.

Once I stopped work I attended the aqua-natal aerobics
session, which was also a source of amusement, as Hilary will
describe later, but all in all I did enjoy the exercise during
pregnancy.

Postnatal exercise, I would say, has been more difficult to get
into the swing of, but of course the rest of the girls and Tim have
always been there to egg me on. I hadn't anticipated that my
new daughter would play such a large role in getting me fit – I
think she is in cahoots with Tim. Basically, Bethan is a little girl
who fights to avoid daytime sleep, as there are far more interesting
things she could be gazing at. My only hope of getting her to
have a daytime rest is for me to put her in the pram and take her
for a walk. After ten or fifteen minutes, her eyes eventually close
and I smile to myself thinking that at last I have cracked it. But
when I turn to go home she always gets one up on me – as soon
as the pram stops, those big blue eyes ping open and start staring
up at me as if to say, 'Why have you stopped, Mummy? I haven't
finished my snooze yet.' So I have to set out again to ensure
she gets a complete rest. To say I walk miles would be an
understatement – I think I could do pram-pushing for England
if only they would introduce it as another obscure Olympic
sport!

In theory, I could have started the aerobic exercise class after
the six-week check, but with my breast abscess and hospitaliz-
ation I did not start until about ten weeks. I also found it difficult
to find the time or inclination to do the exercises that the midwife
gives you immediately after the birth. I wish I had concentrated
on the pelvic-floor ones, though, as once I did start the aerobic
classes at the sports centre, the first time I did a star jump I
was horrified to feel a wet trickle down my leg. Talk about

embarrassment! I felt like putting on one of my daughter's nappies before I attempted that again. Suddenly I found the incentive for those pelvic-floor exercises.

Hilary

* * *

Before becoming pregnant, I was one of those people who love to have a go at all sports. I played hockey for the local club and also frequently enjoyed charging around a squash court, but to say I was sporty would not be very accurate as that implies an element of skill. No, I'm one of those sad characters who has enthusiasm in abundance, but has a skill level of zilch. I played squash two or three times a week, but most people who hadn't picked up a squash racket for half a decade could thrash the pants off me in a match. So it is fortunate, really, that I have always been a very good loser.

Due to my miscarriage scare, I had to give up squash and hockey almost immediately after I fell pregnant. This must have been a big relief to my opponents and team mates, who had been continuing to play with me more out of sympathy and loyalty, I'm sure, than for the challenge. So I took up swimming in order to convince my body not to give up muscle tone altogether. I've never been a great swimmer, but I struggled along at least twice a week and eventually came to enjoy it so much that I decided to have a bash at the aqua-natal aerobics. Now this really was one hell of an experience. I arrived the first time to discover that a third of the main pool was fenced off for this, so Joe Public on the other side was provided with in-pool entertainment from the Fat Ladies Club. Then, not being the brightest of sparks, I stood near the shallow end, which meant that rather than just exposing myself to the viewing public from the shoulders up, my shoulders, arms, breasts and half of my enormous belly and backside all stood nicely proud of the water line. Admittedly, this could have made the exercises exceptionally easy for me, because as everyone else swayed their arms at ninety-degree angles from side to side through the water, mine at a ninety-degree angle were not even skimming the surface! However, in order to gain some benefit from the class and to cover my body mass, but not wanting to draw attention to myself by waddling my way further up the pool, I decided to do the whole class with my knees bent in a sort of wide crouch, like a dog doing its business!

I've never been big on aerobic-type classes, partly because of my own lack of coordination, but largely because I can't stand the stereotypical instructors leaping around with their perfect figures in perfect leggings, with their G-string knickers over the top, showing off their perfect thighs and bums. Not to mention their inane grins – I wonder if they have special classes to teach them how to fix those grins on their perfectly made-up faces for a whole session. Well, if they do, this woman had come out top of the class. Her grin was so huge and fixed, I reckon she had taken out shares in Colgate. As if this was not bad enough, her leaping about in slow motion to depict the restrictions imposed by the force of the water made her look like one of the Flowerpot Men!

One of her favourite exercises was to get us all to run (waddle) as fast as we could in a clockwise circle in the water. Well, little did I realize just how lethal such a simple exercise could be. We all formed a circle, and I took my place in front of two girls who bore a remarkable resemblance to the *Viz* magazine cartoon characters, the Fat Slags. What I did not realize, being no Einstein, is that they would be able to gain momentum at a far greater rate than I would, due to their size – either that or they just had much stronger thigh muscles. Before I knew it, they were overtaking me on the inside. I tell you, if they had not been so intimidating, and if they had not completely knocked me off my feet as they torpedoed past, I reckon I would have got the pool equivalent of road rage!

Well, I definitely learnt from this early experience and I

became determined to try every trick in the book to ensure I kept my head above water in future, especially after the girl next to me announced that her bladder control was not holding out as well as it used to with all the leaping about. So the following week I applied my minimal understanding of physics and took my place in the circle behind the two Fat Slags. This was excellent. I discovered that as long as I managed to stay very close behind them, I had to do hardly any work at all to keep up. It was a bit like Moses' parting of the seas. I had almost got a dry run! However, if I lagged behind, it all went horribly wrong. I then ended up in what amounted to the backlash of the seas crashing back together again, swallowing half the pool and probably the girl-next-to-me's bladder leakages as well!

As D-Day approached, I became very nervous about my waters breaking in the pool. How would I know? Are they a different colour? Would I be able to sneak out or would I have the embarrassment of having to apologize as the whole pool was evacuated? Having discussed these fears with Lyndsey, we came to the conclusion that the mucus plug or 'show' that the midwives kept telling us about would surely come out first. This theory actually offered no comfort but merely conjured up a whole new range of scenarios. What if the *plug* came out while we were swimming? Would it float past? And with a whole pool of pregnant women, would we know if it was ours? The image went through my mind of someone holding up a mucus blob saying, 'Excuse me, I think I've found someone's plug – has anyone lost theirs?' as the rest of the class peered down between their legs to check if it was theirs. As unreal and jovial as this conversation was at the time, it was still enough to put me off going in the pool for the last two weeks before D-Day. The funny thing was, after all the worrying about where we would be when our waters went, not one of the five of us ended up having them go in a spectacular fashion, and most of us waited until we were in the full throes of labour in hospital – boring or what!

As I said before, aerobic-type exercises never were my forte, but I managed to attend the antenatal aerobics regularly and keep up with the routines with minimal trouble. Now, having attended the postnatal aerobic classes, I realize this was not down to my new-found coordination skills, but merely because the exercises were so slow and gentle that even a sloth could have kept up with them. The postnatal classes were a little more lively, to put it mildly. I started attending at the six-week postnatal milestone, and although I did not find it a problem fitness-wise, keeping my boobs from causing me facial injuries and keeping up with the routines was a whole different story. The boobs problem was easily solved with the purchase of what is politely termed an extra-strong sports bra, which strapped my boobs down as though they had been mummified and felt like a steel girdle – very fetching, I'm sure! As for the coordination problem, fortunately or unfortunately (I'm not sure which) Andrea was equally as uncoordinated as I was. Although this gave me a partner in crime to reduce my embarrassment, it also meant that

We bore an uncanny resemblance to a French and Saunders sketch

neither of us had a hope in hell of getting any of the routines right, because if one of us got the hang of things, you could guarantee the other would soon send them off track again. To add to the uncoordinated picture of arms and legs grapevining right when they should have been scooping left, and scooping left when they should have been star-jumping, we were also the two who piled on the weight during our pregnancies, so standing behind the other three with their perfect figures and perfect coordination meant we bore an uncanny resemblance to a French and Saunders sketch!

The whole scene was fairly surreal, with a load of women bouncing about to music while a load of babies looked on, or in my case screamed, from their car seats on the sideline, but Andrea and I have managed to stick at it so far. We have even got the hang of the routines now, so as long as they don't change them I think I will keep going in a vain attempt to tackle the battle of the postnatal bulge and reward myself with that much-needed new underwear.

Sarah

* * *

Before I got pregnant, I had happily got myself into a regular exercise routine of aerobics two to three times a week at the local gym, with mountain biking and walking at weekends. I was eager to continue these pursuits as long as possible into my pregnancy, both in order to maintain myself as a fit and healthy mum-to-be and also to keep those inevitable pregnancy flabby bits at bay. Having spent the past five years working hard to achieve a good level of stamina, I didn't want to lose it suddenly by becoming a pregnant couch potato. One of my overriding concerns, as soon as my pregnancy test proved positive, was not to let myself go to seed. You see so many mothers, as soon as they have had two kids, wandering around like blobs in baggy washed-out tracky bottoms, with unwashed hair and no make-up, as if they cannot be bothered to make themselves look attractive any more. That was not going to be me! Not letting myself go to seed meant continuing regular exercise, eating healthily and maintaining a style of dress that was smart yet not obviously pregnant! Despite my bulge, I was determined to maintain my inner and outer self as far as possible.

I was so keen to carry on exercising, oblivious to my ever-expanding-state, that it took my husband Tim to take me gently to one side after an aerobic session and tell me that my Lycra G-string and leggings were beginning to bulge obscenely, and that the sight was not very becoming for an expectant mother of five months. I think his main concern was that the neighbours, who had not yet been informed of our forthcoming parenthood, might begin to talk about how gross I had become. He was probably worried that they might arrange for the local Weight Watchers representative to pay us a courtesy call. It was at this point that I reluctantly resorted to the purpose-made antenatal exercise classes on Saturday mornings – the Fat Ladies classes, as Tim so aptly nicknamed them. At least everyone in these classes looked pregnant, and it was a strange relief to find myself amongst my own ilk instead of desperately trying to keep up alongside skinny Lycra-clad teenagers.

When I was three months pregnant, Tim's family rented a cottage up in Snowdonia for a week over New Year. We all trooped up to the snowy climes of the northern Welsh hills with walking boots and mountain bikes in tow. My pregnancy at the time was not making itself terribly obvious, either by a protruding bump or persistent morning sickness, so I embarked on all the planned activities with great gusto. The walking I could cope with, albeit taking some of the slopes at a slower pace than usual, but it was the mountain biking that made me realize that my body was not altogether my own. I put it down to the fact that my body was already using a percentage of energy to grow my baby, and not leaving very much spare for me to pump my legs up and down on pedals! Tim enjoys pushing himself to the limits in all physical and mental challenges, so it will be no surprise to anyone that where mountain biking is concerned, he has most fun going cross-country, or, more specifically, off any track marked on the map. I regularly find myself reminding him that I am his wife and not some SAS commando, and that I do not share his love of working my body to the point of exhaustion. On the first bike ride of the holiday (which also proved to be the last), we ended up crossing a marshy field of sheep which had deep dikes cut through it. These dikes provided the challenge Tim was looking for. He was able to take a run at them and leap like a greyhound across the gaps with a mountain bike on each shoulder. Whatever the male urge is that such an achievement satisfies is quite beyond me, but I have become adept at turning a blind eye during the nine years I have known Tim. For my part, however, my sense of humour was being severely put to the test. I was not feeling at peak performance. Temperatures were skimming freezing and I had just endured half an hour's cycle across bumpy grass terrain. I knew it would not be long before my long-suffering acceptance of this ride was going to come to an abrupt end. Following Tim and bikes, I took a flying leap at a dike which was wider than I had anticipated, and as I landed on the other side I fell flat on my face and, of course, on my stomach. Needless to say, a serious sense-of-humour failure resulted. The mixture I felt of rage at being stupid enough to attempt such stunts on frozen ground, and concern about any harm I may have caused my baby, was enough to make me want to storm back to the cottage immediately. The only problem was that we were at least an hour from home, and so I had no choice but to continue. Tim fortunately curtailed the planned route so that we got back earlier.

When reliving my experience with the rest of the family that evening, we of course got worried comments from Tim's parents, to which Tim retorted, 'At least it will make the cord nice and strong so he'll run less risk of falling out.' Now there's a thought

– I wonder if Miriam Stoppard mentions this phenomenon in her books: 'A jolly tough four-hour mountain-bike ride, at approximately the end of the first trimester, will serve to strengthen the attachment of the foetus's umbilical cord. Of course, the bumpier and harder the terrain the better, and a few falls off the bike straight on to your stomach will ensure your baby is born a real tough nut.' I don't think so! Fortunately, I suffered no ill consequences from my tumble, but it did scare me into scaling down my outdoor pursuits slightly.

The amount of exercise I was doing towards the end of pregnancy was well and truly scaled down to swimming only. If you can bear to heave yourself into a swimsuit and parade along the poolside in order to go for a swim, it is worth it. The way the water supports your whole weight is extremely relaxing, but also makes you realize how heavy you are when the time comes to pull yourself up the steps at the end. And this takes me neatly on to the subject of my ever-decreasing swimming costume, something which I would have preferred to leave to the annals of forgotten history, but Hilary and Lyndsey both requested that I mention it.

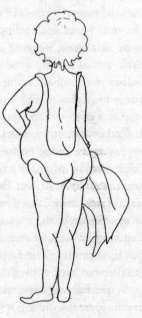

I already had an old black Lycra swimsuit, which I had had for four years. It resembled one of those that you can now buy in maternity format, which stretch ideally in all the right places to accommodate the growing bump. Mine, how-ever, was a bit of an embarrassment. Its elastic was already going, the bum fabric was beginning to perish with age, and it had faded to

*My ever-decreasing
swimming costume*

a delicate shade of bleached grey from too many sunny beach holidays. Added to all this, it was not specifically designed for a pregnant woman, and the deep scooped back proved problematic as time went on. However, I was determined not to buy a brand-new costume when this old one would do perfectly well. There was a price to pay for my reluctance to spend money, though, and each time I hauled myself out of the water I somehow had to simultaneously hold on to the top of my swimsuit to keep my cleavage from plummeting to nipple exposure, and also hold on to the back bit for fear that the over-stretching of the fabric would result in me also exposing my bottom cleavage! I got quite self-conscious about it towards the end of my pregnancy. It's a good job I didn't pass my due date, otherwise I think the swimming-pool attendants would have escorted me from the premises for indecent exposure. Either that, or they would have handed me a copy of the *Sun* and a comb just to make the builder's-bum image complete! The other four were relieved to hear that there was a ceremonial burning of the swimsuit after Jack was born. It really would not have held out for another summer, let alone another pregnancy. If and when the latter happens, I guess I will have to buy a new costume after all.

After Jack was born, I was so eager to get back to my exercise, not only to lose those unwanted pounds but also to build up a sweat again without fear of harming a little person inside me. The five of us began religiously attending the twice-weekly postnatal classes held at the gym, and soon considered ourselves dab hands at the grapevine and star jumps, pelvic floors permitting! No mention of exercise could possibly be made without bringing up the subject of pelvic floors. The pelvic floor seems to be a part of the body that all women are entirely ignorant of until they become pregnant. All of a sudden, everyone around you – midwives, health visitors, doctors, friends, exercise instructors – seems to be talking about them. It wasn't until I began attending the antenatal classes that I really started practising my pelvic-floor exercises regularly, but I soon reached the point where I would find myself sitting in the car, or at work, or even watching TV in the evening, clenching and releasing my insides without being at all conscious of what I was doing. A pattern of twenty short bursts followed by twenty longer clenches seemed to be the routine I had adopted. All I can say is that it certainly pays off to work them good and hard, even if you're not pregnant, because the statistics of women suffering from prolapsed uteruses are frighteningly high, and you are obviously much more vulnerable once you have had a baby. Having spent a good four months practising my pelvic floors during pregnancy, I have now become what you might call an addict, or pelvic-floor junkie.

Andrea

* * *

I have always been a very active person, bordering on being hyperactive. My dad always used to say when I was younger, 'She was born a month early and hasn't stopped rushing ever since,' and he was usually right. I get ever so bored just sitting around the house and always try to keep busy, which was easy before I became pregnant because I would always be taking part in one sport or another. Football involved training twice a week with a game on Sundays. I would usually go to the gym at least once a week, and during the summer it wasn't unusual for me to play tennis every day as well, so when I found out I was pregnant only six games into the football season, what on earth was I going to do? I know now that I could have, and definitely should have, continued with exercise a little longer than I did. At the time, however, I did not want to do anything that might put my unborn child at risk, and going in for crunching tackles on the football pitch was obviously not to be recommended. So I ambled through the first twelve weeks without doing any exercise at all and managed to get on Bruce's nerves in a big way! I was at home so much, and he was so used to having the house to himself whilst I gallivanted off three or four nights a week, that it added a whole new dimension to our relationship actually seeing each other in the evenings! I would have liked to get out more, but much as I did not mind watching my team play matches, watching them train really was not that appealing, even as a means of providing the usual peaceful and tranquil home life for Bruce.

It was meeting Annette at the antenatal classes that encouraged me to start my first pregnancy exercise – swimming. I have a particular hatred of swimming, so this was a strange hobby for me to take up. I actually quite enjoyed swimming as a child, but attending my initial police training course in the late eighties soon put an end to that. They made us swim every single day, but this was not just a leisurely pootle up and down. We were made to get out after each length and do either twenty sit-ups or twenty press-ups, and then jump back in and swim another length. This was a complete nightmare – all dignity went out of the window for the three girls in my class. At first, each time we clambered out we would do all of the usual girlie checks – quickly ensure that our pubes weren't showing, our boobs had not escaped and our costumes hadn't nestled up our backsides. How-ever, with the horrible police training instructor shouting 'Same pay, same pain, Miss' every time we flagged behind, we soon just forgot about dignity and got on with it. It was with some trepidation, therefore, that I agreed to go swimming with Annette. I was very relieved to find that she was on my wavelength as we bobbed gently up and down the pool, opting for the five-minute chat after every length instead of the twenty sit-ups! We felt ever so pleased with ourselves if we managed just five lengths in our half-hour session, and afterwards we would obviously have worked up an appetite and would have to reward ourselves by indulging in a snack of some sort from the sports-centre café.

Apart from swimming, the only other exercise I took during pregnancy was the occasional walk along a local canal with Bruce. During the latter stages this became a bit of a problem on the tow-path, though, which in certain places is only wide enough for two very slender people. This was all right when it was just Bruce and me on the tow-path, although admittedly walking in single file is not exactly romantic, but the problems arose when we met other canal strollers coming from the opposite direction. When they saw my bulk heading towards them, we often saw panic spreading over their faces as they quickly went into reverse and found a safe passing point for me to trundle past. I think these poor innocent passers-by lived in fear of ending up in the murky slime that is politely termed canal water. I don't think the life-saving skills that I learnt at the training centre would have proved particularly successful at this stage in my pregnancy, although my buoyancy aids (boobs) may have at least acted as a satisfactory life raft until help arrived! For fear of causing injury to others, I refrained from any exercise at all after thirty-five weeks, deciding I would make up for it after the birth.

Once Max arrived, I could not wait for the six-week check-up so that I could get back to my sport. In fact I did cheat and go for a run after about five weeks, but I realized that night why you are told to wait until six weeks, when I suffered a fair amount of pain in the pelvic region. After getting the go-ahead from my GP when Max was six weeks old, I finally played my first ninety minutes in a friendly reserve football match. I thought to myself, 'Nine months out can't make *that* much difference – I might not be fit but I've still got my natural ability.' After thirty seconds I was nearly dying, and as I briefly bent forward to catch my breath, the attacker I was supposed to be marking unsuspectingly snuck past me and scored a goal in the first minute. It was only then that it dawned on me just how out of shape I was. The sad thing was that Annette had brought Gavin and Emily to watch me play, because she had never seen a ladies' match. I don't think she was too impressed with what she saw, and she has politely refrained from coming along again! Since that day I have trained, trained and trained some more, and I have played in every match so far for the reserves. I scored my first goal last week and felt on top of the world when the ball hit the back of the net.

I also attend postnatal aerobics, which, as Hilary has said, is not exactly my cup of tea. Everything she says about my coordination is one hundred per cent accurate. Give me a football to keep in the air with my knees or feet, no problem, but ask my arms and legs to perform two different tasks simultaneously, and to music, and I am completely lost. I have to admit, my main reason for attending these classes was initially for the social aspect of meeting up with the others, but having always mocked aerobic-type girlies, I am embarrassed to admit now that I actually quite enjoy the classes. And having managed to get the hang of things, I am now proud to say that I am no longer the worst person there.

My final effort at exercise came after some advice from an assistant in the local sports shop. He said that while I push the pram around town I should wear these special weights on my ankles. Being a complete mug, I duly purchased a pair, and looked like an absolute idiot waddling around with huge Velcro-strapped sand-filled ankle weights that make a scrunching noise with every step. I would certainly be noticed if I strolled around town with them on, as everyone would both hear and see me coming, in my scrunching go-faster fluorescent ankle accessories. Most people peer into your pram, not ogle at your ankles, so I decided that this was a spectacle I did not need to make of myself! Never mind, I suppose they will at least come in handy for use as sandbags next time the British weather strikes our doorstep, but until then, they have joined my maternity cossie in the loft.

Annette

***

When it comes to exercise, I would describe myself as someone with good intentions but lacking in motivation. I have always perceived exercise as something I suppose I should do rather than something I really enjoy. And when I had a choice of whether to do some exercise or do something else, such as shopping, exercise would come a sad second and I could always justify putting it off until tomorrow. My favourite excuse was that I worked long hours, was too busy and did not have the time or energy. Prior to pregnancy, the only exercise I undertook was walking, the occasional swim and the once-in-a-blue-moon trip to the gym. When I did force myself to partake in these activities, I actually enjoyed them and felt a sense of achievement. I would promise myself that I must do this again soon, but I never did, especially when it was up to me to motivate myself. What a lazy cow!

However, once I fell pregnant my attitude changed slightly. I read a few magazines and books about my developing unborn child, and they all said that exercise was good for the baby. I therefore worried that if I did not exercise I would not be doing the best for my child. At last, I had found a way of motivating myself, so the next step was to decide how I was going to exercise. I popped down to the local sports centre to see what antenatal classes were available, and to check out the swimming times. The only things that took my fancy were a Saturday-morning antenatal aerobics class, and a Monday-evening water-aerobics class.

My first challenge was swimming. I managed to persuade Andrea to come along with me to the water aerobics. I had an ulterior motive in arranging to meet Andrea, as I knew that there would be no escape if I had a companion with me. We turned up in our sexy maternity costumes, to be greeted by a horrified instructor. She was a trendy young woman with a perfect figure and fashionable aerobics kit to go with it, and, just to complete the look, she wore a telephonist-style headphone-microphone just to make sure she really could leap about without any restrictions. This young lady was not happy about having two pregnant women in her class, and did not really know what to do with us. She reluctantly let us join in, on the understanding that we took it steady and did not over-exert ourselves. Andrea and I found this most amusing, as we had absolutely no intention of doing too much! With this in mind, we had visions of a hard work-out and not being able to keep up with the pace. However, when we saw the rest of the class, we realized that youth was on our side, and that many of the women were carrying the same amount of weight around with them as we were, but without the excuse! We proceeded to bob up and down and swim round in circles for the next hour. The highlight of the evening was synchronized swimming. It's just a shame we didn't have the statutory flowery swim-hats and nose-clips. We had to split into groups of ten, and five people in each group would float on their backs whilst the other five pulled them round in a circle. Of course no one really wanted to come near us two antenatal aliens, but one group eventually took pity on us and reluctantly allowed us to synchron-ize with them. We must have looked a complete picture, floating on our backs with our stomachs protruding from the water like beached whales.

Though we had coped well with the class, we did struggle with the jumping up and down. You do not feel pregnant when your bump is underwater, as the weight is well supported. But when you jump up a fraction too high and the bump rises above the surface, you really know you are pregnant. We therefore decided that we would not attend any more of these classes and would stick to basic swimming.

I arranged to meet Andrea once a week to go swimming. I was determined not to let her down by not turning up, and I thought that as she was the sporty type she would also be the reliable type and would make me go. We kept this up on and off for about ten weeks, until we were both about thirty weeks pregnant. In the last few weeks, though, there would always be a message on my answer-machine from Andrea when I rushed home from work to meet her at the pool, with a convincing excuse why she could not attend. Her excuses started off being quite original, such as having a strange rash and not wanting the chlorine to aggravate it (it later turned out to be the onset of her stretch marks), but later her excuses diminished to being quite simply 'just too tired', which was a condition I fully sympathized with. Needless to say, I was not at all disappointed at her not wanting to attend. Her justification then became my justification and I would not venture on the swimming trip by myself.

At around thirty weeks I bravely decided to attend Flash Your Knickers Fiona's aqua-natal aerobics class, which was run at a leisure centre. I turned up early, changed into my costume and waddled out into the pool area. Having never been here before, what I had not accounted for was the fact that it is a state-of-the-art place with palm trees everywhere, wave machines, and mini-bridges linking the different pools. I could not see Flash Your Knickers Fiona anywhere, and I was just about to make a hasty

Certainly not how I would want to make my modelling debut

retreat when a lifeguard obviously guessed my mission and pointed me towards a group of coconut trees in the far corner. In order to make my way over to the class I had to cross the centre bridge, displaying my delightful figure to all and sundry. It was just my luck, too, that a photo-shoot was going on, with elegant, *slim* models being snapped in new swimwear *en route* to my desired destination, meaning that I had to waddle my way right past them! To this day, I still dread turning over the pages of a magazine to find a beautiful, slender model posing by a palm tree in a lovely, trendy costume, and there in the background my contrasting pregnant bulk trying to sneak past unnoticed. I have never really had any illusions of becoming a model, but if I had this is certainly not how I would want to make my debut.

Having overcome this hurdle, I then turned right at the whirlpool and was suddenly faced with the sight of Flash Your Knickers Fiona prancing around in a purple leotard. As you can imagine from our previous descriptions, this was not her most flattering attire. Her stomach was protruding so that she looked more like a member of the antenatal class than the instructor, and to top it off, she was in desperate need of a bikini-line wax. She certainly was not a good advert for what the class could help you achieve with your figure and I kept thinking to myself, 'Thank God the others are not here to see this.' It would have been very difficult to take the class seriously if I had had a partner in crime to witness the spectacle.

It took me until I was thirty-two weeks to get myself organized and turn up to the Saturday-morning antenatal aerobics class, and even then I only really turned up out of curiosity. I had arranged to meet Lyndsey, who was attending these classes quite regularly, but it was somewhat disastrous for me, because the instructor made such a fuss about me starting exercising so late into my pregnancy that I was too intimidated to turn up again.

I gave up work at thirty-eight weeks, by which time I was not fit for anything beyond lifting a cup of raspberry-leaf tea to my lips. So I justified a break from exercise for a while.

Sex?!

This has to have been the hardest chapter to write. It was one thing having an open and honest girlie gossip about our sex lives over a glass of wine, safe in the knowledge that all that was said was contained within those four walls. Actually opening up our sex lives for public viewing, so to speak, is a different matter altogether. After all, our mums will be reading this and, heaven forbid, our dads too! However, no matter how hard the task has been, we have all bared our souls, and here goes for as much detail as we are brave enough to give. I am afraid you will have to read between the lines for the rest!

Sex in pregnancy and after pregnancy is definitely one of the biggest worries for most women. How will things change? How will I cope? How will my partner cope? Sex is the thing that gets us all into this state, and the thing that can change the most as a result. The impact of a baby on a relationship is hard enough to grasp, so the prospect of that baby possibly damaging or at least changing the sexual part of the relationship is a realistic and understandable fear. I am not sure if we are going to alleviate those fears with our tales, but the simple fact that we have got something to say on this subject must at least offer some reassurance that it does not all end when the new life begins!

Annette

***

I have always considered myself lucky to have had an active sex life – however, the month we decided to try to conceive, things went to the extreme and we were most definitely over-active!

Gavin and I were determined to hit the jackpot, and once it had been confirmed that we had done, it took us over a month to recover – we were both absolutely shattered, so we took a break. About this time, I was also the victim of morning sickness and fatigue, so there were no complaints from my corner!

Unfortunately, this little break lasted a bit longer than I had anticipated, as Gavin was playing hard to get. He was put off by the fact that there would be three of us present, and this did not feel quite right to him. He was also frightened of harming the baby, and despite my reassurances and references to Miriam Stoppard's bible of childbirth, he would still not believe me. I remember feeling a little frustrated and thinking that this was going to be a long pregnancy! Eventually his hormones got the better of him and we went back to normal for a while.

Our main problem was the size of my stomach. I have to say that I did not feel particularly attractive during pregnancy. I felt fat, knackered, spotty and frumpy. Looking back, this seems a little silly, as whenever I see a pregnant woman now I think how wonderful and radiant she looks. But good old Gavin, no matter how much larger my knickers got, he just did not seem to mind. We had to experiment a little to establish comfort, however, and when I only had four weeks to go until my due date we decided to slow things down and settled for once a week only.

As my due date approached and the excitement and anticipation mounted, Andrea's due date came and went with no sign of a baby. She told me that she had even tried sex to induce labour, so Gavin and I took this as our cue to do likewise. I am not entirely sure why, because it obviously hadn't worked for her! When this failed, I then tried having my legs and bikini line waxed, as I thought that there was a slim chance that pain and shock to the system might induce labour. Of course, that did not work either, but my legs looked great! It was extremely difficult to have the back of my legs done, though, because, unable to lie on my front as usual, I had to adopt the crouching-on-all-fours pose with one leg sticking bolt out behind me. The waxing of my bikini line was even more of a spectacle. Imagine an extremely heavily pregnant woman contorting herself on a pink padded couch, while the beautician looks quizzically at my bump. Legs firstly spread in a butterfly to wax the upper bikini line, and then bent up either side of the bump to get at the lower bikini line. I felt so embarrassed, but although it sadly did not induce the much-hoped-for labour, it did give me practice of my birthing position. Five months on I am now trying to pluck up courage to return to the same beautician to have my legs waxed again – or perhaps I'll just change beauty salon to save embarrassment all round.

When I finally went into labour and gave birth, my first thought was that I was never ever going to be up to having sex again. I felt like I had run a marathon and had been abused in an unspeakable manner. I thought I would never recover. Combined with this was the hard realization during the first few weeks of Emily's life that I had to survive on less sleep, and not only find the time to look after Emily, but look after myself as well. Sex was way down in my priorities.

Having produced this perfect miracle together, I felt a deep sense of pride in both Gavin and myself for this huge achievement. We would each look on with adoration as the other kissed Emily good night and we would then nestle into our bed feeling the happiest people alive. Naturally, I craved the affection of an intimate cuddle to seal this scene of satisfaction and would snuggle up close to Gavin, wrapping my arms around him. Before I knew it, that tell-tale sign of stimulation would be prodding at my side and the romantic image would be blown as a row ensued, with him accusing me of teasing when I refused to oblige, and me accusing him of lacking compassion for the ordeal my body had been through. Nothing short of a bolster down the centre of the bed, preventing any possibility of misunderstood body contact, would have cured the situation! Why is it that men can't just cuddle?

When Emily was four weeks old, though, I began to feel like

a human being again, and once Andrea had let slip that she and Bruce had successfully performed the act, I thought that Gavin and I should try and return to normality, so we gave it a go. I have to say that this first attempt felt very awkward and clumsy, and I was so worried about falling pregnant that it took a lot of the enjoyment away, but now, two months later, things are back to pre-pregnancy status. The hardest problem for me now is remembering to take the Pill again!

Sarah

* * *

By the time I reached my due date, I was beginning to think that my pregnancy had been an immaculate conception, so long in the dim and distant past was the memory of Tim and I ever having bonked. Tim's continued absence during the week, combined with both his and my aversion to sex whilst I looked like a beached whale when naked, made for a monk-like existence during the latter months of pregnancy. I certainly had no desire whatsoever to wear sexy underwear (assuming I would have been able to fit into it anyway), and, as I was not even able to see below my belly button towards the end, the thought of sex in that state was laughable. It is a shame, though, that my expanded chest could not have been put to better use – what a waste!

According to a story I read in the only *Mother and Baby* magazine I bought during my pregnancy, Tim and I were by no means the norm. This article outlined several couples' attitudes to sex during pregnancy, or could more appropriately be called the 'Perfect Paul and Super Sue guide to pregnant sex'. The Perfect Pauls, if not positively turned on by their pregnant women, enjoying exploring different positions to accommodate the larger stomach, were at the very least sympathetic and keen to indulge in heavy petting to satisfy their partners' sexual urges during pregnancy. As for the women, all of those interviewed admitted to feeling a heightened sexuality whilst being pregnant and were experiencing more intense orgasms. All I can say is, 'Bully for you, Sue!' I hated them all for making me feel inadequate and lacking in an obviously crucial side to my femininity. It was a shame that I hadn't yet met my four mates, who would have reassured me straight away that I was not an oddity. I mean, let's face it, if we were all able to pose Demi Moore-like in *Vanity Fair* whilst heavily pregnant, then maybe we'd feel more confident prancing around semi-naked in front of the bedroom mirror, excitedly enticing our husbands with cries of 'Chase me, chase me!'

Even the maintenance of pubic hair in late pregnancy became a challenge for the weak-hearted. Determined as I was not to go into hospital to have my baby with an untidy bikini line, I set about it with a razor blade, blindly trimming away where man had feared to tread for the past five months. I remembered that Flash Your Knickers Fiona had mentioned shaving down below using a mirror, but I had unfortunately got into the bath that night without thinking about rummaging through my make-up bag for a small mirror. All I had to guide me was my memory. I caught a glimpse of myself in the full-length mirror as I stepped out of the bath, and was aghast at the result of my endeavours. Bald and tufty is probably the best description! But what else could I do with an obstruction as large as a spacehopper preventing me from bending over any further? I had once broached with Tim the possibility of him helping me out with shaving my legs (another thing that Perfect Paul was prepared to do for his partner). Tim's middle name unfortunately isn't Paul, and he wasn't keen to get his diary out and mark a date for shaving my legs, so I'm sure that he wouldn't have been an eager volunteer for the rest.

We left it a good ten weeks before we attempted sex after Jack was born. It had been a blessing that Tim had been away in Spain during the week, and at weekends we were both too tired to contemplate more than just a cuddle in bed. A work colleague of mine once boasted that he and his wife had bonked just two weeks after their son was born. She was a braver woman than me. All I can say is that I was quite happy to let the guy proudly hold on to that record! When Tim took the month of August off as holiday to renovate our house, I was secretly thankful that he was working himself so physically hard doing all this DIY that he had no energy left to consider anything else! In the meantime, I was interested to notice that my cycle kicked back into play, and that my periods began again about two months after I had given up breastfeeding. However, despite feeling quite frisky again when I was at my most fertile, the mere thought of using tampons again made me go weak at the knees, let alone anything more adventurous!

When, at last, we did tackle the dastardly deed again, I was expecting it to be a very easy, albeit slightly sore, experience. It was certainly sore, but what surprised me was that it was much, much tighter than I was expecting, I felt like a virgin all over again! Fortunately, things got back to normal relatively quickly, but I was paranoid about getting pregnant again so soon, so we took every precaution going. Initially, 'plastic macs' as well as abstention during my fertile period were the necessary forms of birth control, but I knew that the sooner I got back on the Pill, the safer I was going to be. I guess I'll just have to postpone the joys of mucus testing again until a later date. As I mentioned earlier, my persistence with the pelvic-floor exercises certainly paid off as far as continence is concerned, but I wonder if the strength of my pelvic-floor muscle is also responsible for the tightness I experienced the first time Tim and I ventured back into sex. Tim says that my grip is now so tight that if ever we're short of cash we could always move to Thailand, where he's sure I could earn a decent wage in some of the less salubrious clubs, using ping pong balls and darts as props!

Lyndsey

* * *

If I had left this page blank, as the others suggested, it would more or less tell the whole story from conception to present day. But, to be fair, the picture isn't quite as bleak as that.

The only desire I felt was to smash those blasted mirrored doors

At the realization that I was pregnant, the tables certainly turned from the sublime to the ridiculous. Whilst the foetus was growing to the size of a fingernail, I was just about crawling to my bed at night on hands and knees, as I felt so exhausted. The mornings were no better, as they were blessed with the ritual of making a dash to the toilet to throw up, so I think it is fair to say that during those early months my sex drive took a plummet.

Also, as my body physically adapted to its new role of carrying a child, I found the resulting aching boobs and big fat belly a huge turn off, and the only desire that I felt was to smash those blasted mirrored wardrobe doors, which seemed to follow me wherever I went in the bedroom. Tim, however, throughout my pregnancy restrained me from taking the axe to the mirrors, and reassured me that he did not find my new shape repulsive, but found it fascinating and desirable. On those few Saturday mornings when Tim brought breakfast to me, before the nausea took over, we did manage a couple of bonks which were like no other. No, there was no bondage or swinging from the light bulbs, but the mere fact that we could have carefree sex without worrying about me becoming pregnant was a turn-on in itself, strange as it may seem.

As the weeks rolled by and the flutters in my tummy arrived, I started to feel slightly better and in a weak moment would flirt with the idea of sex. By this stage, however, the proverbial horse had bolted, as now Tim felt uncomfortable with the idea of making love for fear of harming or interfering with the unborn child. Of course, this escalated as my bump increased in size, and I think we were both secretly hoping that I wouldn't go over my due date because, no matter what the old wives suggest, the thought of sex at such a late stage was a prospect that neither of us wanted to consider.

Following Bethan's birth, the last thing I wanted to think about was sex, for a number of reasons. Firstly, it was the last thing on my mind in those early weeks, when all my energy was spent feeding, nursing and caring for the newborn. Then the mastitis struck, which plagued me for four weeks, and the final straw was the huge gaping wound on my left boob following the abscess removal. Never mind not feeling sexy during pregnancy, this was a corker. Again, Tim reassured me that it wasn't that bad, but this was only as long as he didn't actually have to see the open wound. He would run a mile should I so much as feign taking off the dressing. In fact, this became a useful weapon when

Tim did have any sexual desires and I wasn't in the mood. All I had to do was drop my dressing and he'd bolt out of bed, quick as a flash, not to be seen for dust. The day came when the wound had closed up and the dressing was no longer required. I pinned him to the floor and watched him squirm as I unbuttoned my blouse to show him my scar. He wriggled as if I was going to torture him, but as soon as he saw it a sigh of relief went through his body and he proclaimed, 'Oh, it's not *that* bad, it'll soon disappear.'

One of my other fears about making love was how was it going to feel, having given birth to a thirty-eight-centimetre-circumference head, and would it be the same as before? I had heard the expression, 'It's like throwing a pencil into a bucket,' so I was quite taken aback to find it the complete opposite. I think on Bethan's exit my body must have contracted to such an extent as if to say, 'You ain't coming back this way.' To say it was a tight squeeze would be putting it mildly – perhaps the expression should be, 'It's like fitting a pencil into a drinking straw'! After so many months of celibacy, it has been like starting from scratch again, which has definitely added to the thrill, but this time there is a new form of contraception. Yes, that little blue-eyed baby flashes into my mind at the height of passion, and I hear myself cry, 'Don't forget the condom!'

Andrea

***

You may remember my friend Lizzie, whom I mentioned earlier. She was the one who was brave enough to accompany me to the antenatal classes and was extremely put off pregnancy by what she discovered at them. Well, she was totally and utterly put off the prospect of ever having a baby when she found out that I went a good five months without sex during my pregnancy. She can only just about manage to go five hours without a bonk, and could not begin to entertain the thought of going five whole months!

I don't know if it is the same with other couples, but our sex life has been through various stages during our relationship. After Bruce and I first started courting we were at it like rabbits, then when we moved in together it went down to around twice a week, and finally after tying the knot it settled down to a civilized average of once a week. The severe deterioration in our sex life during pregnancy, it has to be said, was a bit of a shock. At first, I wouldn't let Bruce near me, due to my paranoia about harming the unborn child. Next came the morning sickness – the thought of having to stop halfway through to run to the toilet and puke did not seem particularly romantic, so my vow of celibacy remained. Then, finally, there was my ever-expanding body size, which repulsed me so much that I was sure Bruce would not be too excited by my new additional curves and bumps, with the exception of my boobs, of course! So yet again nookie was off limits. Well, with the paranoia and morning sickness lasting up until about twenty weeks and my fatness becoming a problem from around twenty-five weeks, I am sure you can work out that this actually only left five weeks mid-pregnancy for any sexual activity whatsoever. We did manage to fit in a couple of sessions in those few weeks, and fortunately they were ones to remember. The combination of mid-pregnancy bloom, carefree, condom-free passion and the long abstention which had preceded these weeks sent us back to the early days of our relationship with stacks of sensual stuff. Unfortunately, this new-found sexual state was very short-lived, and celibacy soon took over again.

One thing I can say is that I have never been one to plan when to have sex. We have never exactly sat down, plotted out when we would tackle our weekly bonks and written the dates in our diary. It was always a bit more spontaneous than that, with romantic meals and nights out usually preceding the passionate event. Bruce rarely came to bed at the same time as me, he always liked staying up until around midnight, so mornings were the favoured time for us. However, I have to confess that during the latter stages of my pregnancy we had to resort to planning a couple of 'events'. Basically, as my due date came and went, I was getting pretty pissed off with life, just waddling around the house all day and waiting. In desperation, we decided to put the old wives' tale about the three Hs to the test, these being a hot curry (not a problem, as I have always eaten at least one a week), a hot bath (again no big deal as I usually have one a day), and finally a hot, steamy, passionate sex session. So we both somewhat reluctantly agreed that if I got to one week overdue we would resort to this. As it turned out, this was going to create a problem. We managed the sex part, the problem was that there was just no way you could call it hot, steamy or passionate. The session was planned and carried out with military precision. Bruce was just about a willing participant, mainly through fear for his own safety, as I was getting so large he thought I might roll over and flatten him in his sleep. Having made these plans, putting them into action was another matter. The missionary position was definitely out of the question. It would have been impossible for us even to attempt it. I had read about doing it with me lying on my side, but I found this most uncomfortable and there was absolutely no way I was going to do it 'doggy style', even if I had gone a month overdue. Well, without the aid of the Kama Sutra to assist us, we opted for trial and error and eventually settled for 'girls on top' as the only plausible and relatively dignified possibility. I dread to think what Max must have thought looking out from inside – I had visions of his head 'bish-boshing' up and down, which did nothing for my concentration on the task in hand! No matter what he thought of the event, though, it obviously did not encourage him to leave home, so we had to go through it all again! Retrospectively, I realize now that I was actually quite relieved that it was so unsuccessful. The thought of going into hospital in labour only hours after having sex and the midwife finding all the evidence when she gave me an internal examination would have been so unbelievably embarrassing. I don't think Bruce would have had the bottle to stay with me through labour if he'd thought the midwife had known what we had been up to!

I was unfortunate to need stitches after Max's arrival, and did not think that I would ever be able to entertain Bruce's tackle in that area again! However, just like for any other wound, time is a great healer, so three to four weeks later we started thinking about it. I was desperate to find out if I was still in one piece and whether or not Bruce would find it different. I had heard so many wisecracks from male police colleagues during my pregnancy about how a woman is never the same after giving birth. They were coming out with jibes like, 'Don't forget to tell Bruce to get the midwife to put an extra stitch in for him.' This constant banter had stuck in my memory and I wanted to find out for myself as soon as possible. Also I had, after all, conceived and given birth first out of our gang, so it was seen as my responsibility to take the plunge first so that the others could follow. It was around the four-week postnatal stage that we gave it a go, and it's sad to say that we did actually plan it again. I won't go into vast detail but we managed it gently, and Bruce diplomatically announced that it did not feel any different for him. I wish I could say the same. It was almost ruined when the baby walkie-talkie thing sprung to life with Max crying halfway through, but the little lad must have had a sixth sense that this was not a convenient time to join us, as he coughed a couple of times and went back to sleep.

Three months on, I am pleased to say that our sex life is back to its pre-pregnancy state – well, almost. Bruce gets so tired with this fatherhood lark that he now actually comes to bed at the same time as me, so I think that things may have even got better. We certainly don't need to plan sex, anyway! Who knows, with this new-found knowledge, Lizzie may even consider having a child yet. After all, she's had enough practice.

Hilary

* * *

After twelve years together, I would not have described our pre-pregnancy sex life as exactly rampant. We had what I would describe as a healthy as opposed to a rampant sex life! This gradually decreased as the bump increased and now, four months after Molly's birth, our sex life is not exactly sick, but it is definitely under the weather.

I would like to be able to blame this on sleep deprivation or discomfort, but neither would be true, and it is not down to lack of interest either. I think the main stumbling block at the moment is actually this book. I spend many an evening writing and often work into the early hours of the morning because this is the only time of the day that I am Molly-free. David, however, starts work at seven in the morning, and therefore he is out for the count by the time I get to bed. The poor chap will be very grateful when this whim, as he thinks of it, is finished. So as you are reading this now, I hope that means we will have regained our pre-pregnancy pleasurable sex life again.

Sex in pregnancy varied greatly at the different stages. In the beginning, before we actually knew, we had an extremely rampant week in Paris. As my period was late, we took every day as a plus and lived life to the full thinking that the next day it would all be off limits. As a result, this turned out to be a holiday which only our honeymoon could top for sexual activity, as obviously the curse never arrived!

Unfortunately, with the miscarriage scare that followed a week later, our sex life then took a nose-dive, with my body being completely off-limits until the twenty-four-week survival zone. The doctor assured us that we could have gentle sex, but as neither of us was entirely sure how you defined sex as gentle or not gentle, we chose abstinence as the safer option.

After week twenty-four, we decided it was time to have a go again, in case we forgot how! Sex became an occasional event only, and was definitely sex and not love-making. My body image was so horrendous that I laid down huge lists of new rules. No lights on, no touching my fat arse, no kissing anywhere other than my face, etc. It was a bit like a crystal-maze challenge for David to work out how to achieve the eventual goal through all of the obstacles I was putting in his way! By thirty-four weeks, my list of nos was so long that the challenge was deemed impossible. I could not bear any of my body parts to be seen by then. The water retention had taken hold so badly that even my fingers and toes bore an uncanny resemblance to packets of pork-farmers' sausages. I was so blown up with fluid that I reckon if someone had stuck a pin in me half a dozen times they could have hired me out as a temporary fountain feature at social events!

In addition to my self-disgust destroying our sex lives, the involvement of Molly from the inside was another huge turn-off. There was so much activity within and my stomach would go so hard, it was almost as though the poor baby could feel the action starting like an earthquake and was carrying out her safety procedures. She quickly put up scaffolding to prevent her ceiling from caving in and then adopted the aeroplane crash position by pointing her bony little bum up through my belly button! As you can imagine, this vivid visual image I managed to conjure up did absolutely nothing for my arousal!

Despite all of this, we too managed the obligatory bonk on the day Molly was due. Being the last to give birth, I was desperate for my baby to come out and tried all of the old wives' tales, to no avail. I wish I had been brave enough to ask Annette and Andrea if they had tried it before we tackled the task. It might have saved us the effort if I had known of its poor success rate in advance! Everything they say is true, too – there is no way sex at forty weeks pregnant can be described as anything other than a functional task, and I think that any man who succeeds in this mission deserves a medal for services beyond the call of duty. As for Bruce, tackling the task twice, he deserves nothing short of the Victoria Cross!

During the first week after Molly was born, I bounced back to life with a vengeance. I had never felt so good. My water retention started to go within hours of her birth and gradually, as that first week went by, my face halved in size, my fingers and toes re-emerged and I had ankles again! I felt so good that I started leaping about, going for long walks and doing things, anything, everything. I felt great. I even had thoughts about having a bash at bonking again, but thought better of it quite quickly! Well, I came crashing down to earth with a thud when the midwife was checking my numerous stitches and pointed out that gravity was taking its toll and the scar tissue was all a bit loose. It felt as though I had a half-in, half-out tampon between my legs, but in fact it was my own dangling flesh. She recommended that I do one hundred pelvic-floor-muscle exercises a day and lie down with my feet and bottom slightly raised. The thought of my bits permanently dangling out led me to take this advice *big time*. I actually opted for one thousand pelvic-floor-muscle exercises minimum, and did head stands to make sure everything slipped back to its rightful home! I was so disgusted and frightened by all of this that I could not bear even to have a look or feel down there myself to see what was going on, let alone let David anywhere near.

Five weeks after Molly was born, I returned to the doctor to have it all checked out again. After the doctor had had a good poke around, she asked whether I had resumed my sex life. '*Certainly not*,' I claimed affrontedly, thinking she was going to apportion blame for my war wounds on over-zealous sexual activities being resumed too early, but no. 'Well, I think the best thing you can do is go away and resume your sex life, because that is the best way to get that lot healing,' she announced, pointing between my legs, and sent me packing with my mouth hanging open and a prescription for the Mini-Pill and KY jelly! She also ordered me to return in three weeks for a re-check.

David had fearfully anticipated that surgery might be the recommended cure I returned with, so you can imagine his absolute delight when he discovered that I had been prescribed sex, and he dutifully offered his services!

I think we were both a bit nervous about tackling our first post-childbirth bonk, although we did not discuss these fears beforehand. The badly healing war wounds, in addition to general fear about what it would feel like, definitely created an element of trepidation for both of us. This first sexual encounter certainly wasn't an amazingly pleasurable experience, but it wasn't so drastic that it put me off completely! I don't know exactly how many bonks we were supposed to have in those three weeks, but two days before my appointment we had still only managed one. We have both always been the sort of people who are up burning the midnight oil the night before an assignment is due in, and this assignment was no exception. We managed to squeeze three more sessions in during the last two days, and I was given the all-clear, having healed to the point of a diagnosis of perfection, at my next appointment!

As I said earlier, our sex life remains a little erratic, but hopefully it will soon improve when this books stops eating into our bed time and Mollyless moments. The limitations of our current sex life were summarized by poor David recently when we were talking about having a second child. I suggested that maybe we should start trying again somewhere around Molly's first birthday and David's face lit up. 'Great,' he said. 'You mean I will get sex again in eight months' time?' So you can imagine how chuffed he was when I pointed out that both his birthday and Christmas fell before then!

The Big Day – the Moment We've All Been Waiting For

Labour has to be the best-kept secret of womanhood, and we have no intention of breaking it now. We don't actually think it would be possible to do this anyway, because no matter how good a command of the English language we have, putting the experience of labour into words is a task we have deemed impossible.

Throughout pregnancy, all you hear are other women's tales of labour. How many hours they were in labour, how many stitches they had, what pain relief they required and so on. No matter how many tales you sit through, though, no one can actually tell you what labour is going to be like for *you*. Nobody can tell you how much pain *you* will be in, what pain relief *you* will require or how magical that moment will be when *your* baby finally puts in an appearance. Horror stories of horrendous labours are just what you do not need when the experience of your first-ever one is imminent. After all, what went in has got to come out! Thousands of women go through this experience every day and not only live to tell the tale, but actually put themselves in the predicament of going through the experience a second and third time, so on this basis alone there is no point in panicking in advance. At the end of the day, it is going to happen whether you worry about it or not, although admittedly not worrying is easier said than done.

So what are we going to write in this chapter, then? Well, we decided to focus on some of the more amusing moments in our labours – yes, it is not all pain and panting, which hopefully our anecdotes will help you to realize.

Andrea

* * *

This is the one occasion when I finally get to say that I came off lightly, because my labour and birth really were not that bad at all! My official time in established labour was recorded as three and a half hours, which is pretty good. I've put it down to all the excess fat on my body at the time, which I reckon must have somehow cushioned the blow! Seriously, though, at no stage did I ever think I wouldn't go through it again, nor did I do any of the traditional swearing at my husband for getting me there in the first place. Don't get me wrong, it wasn't the most pleasant experience I have been through, but it was not as bad as I'd been led to believe.

As the due date approached, passed and disappeared into distant memory, the excitement and anticipation soon faded into daily devastation at the prospect of facing yet another twenty-four hours without the baby's arrival. By the time I was nearly two weeks late, I had given up excitement completely and was just counting down to the inducement date. Similarly, Bruce had given up on the idea of an *au naturel* onset, and ended up getting up each morning for work as though labour were not even a possibility in his daily schedule. So when my waters broke in bed one morning, it actually came as a complete shock to us both. Bruce was getting dressed when I suddenly became aware of a warm sensation on my legs. I quickly did a mental check of all the possibilities. It could not be a leaking pipe, it was definitely under the covers. I had not got a hot-water bottle, and I certainly had not wet myself, which only left one possibility. *This was it!* As I was doing this quick mental check, I gradually became aware of Bruce's contribution to this, the most magical moment of our lives. The arrival of our first-born was now imminent, but unaware of this he was sitting on the edge of the bed, whinging on and on about his bloody socks! What a magical memory! Apparently, I had washed his wool-based socks at too high a temperature and they had shrunk. Poor love! He was instructing me on my use of the washing machine for future sock-washes when, with just four simple words, I decided to send him flying off his sock-shrinking soap-box and into a state of parenthood panic. 'My waters have broken.' The poor chap catapulted off the bed. Suddenly socks were the furthest things from his thoughts. I think he would have settled for a pair of silk stockings in his bid to complete the dressing process as fast as possible. It must have been something to do with the helplessness of the situation, but Bruce's reaction to the onset of labour was one of the most comical scenes I have ever witnessed. It was like watching one of those memorable Benny Hill chases, when they speed up the film. It just needed the music to go with it.

As it turned out, there was absolutely no need for Bruce to rush – he would have had enough time to have hand-knitted himself half a dozen pairs of socks before the arrival of Max! We went into hospital, but as I was not having any contractions, and they were a little over-crowded, I was sent home and told to 'keep clean'. Keep clean – what the hell does that mean? I had absolutely no intention of embarking on a display of mud wrestling at this stage, but having read all the bumph on the risk of infection entering the womb once the waters have broken, I decided that I was not going to take any chances. I spent almost the whole of the next twelve hours in the bath, emptying a little out and topping it up with warm water as the temperature dropped every twenty minutes or so. By early afternoon, I still was not having any contractions and Bruce was getting a little concerned for my skin. It had progressed a stage further than prune-like and now bore a closer resemblance to a raisin! For fear of me shrivelling up completely, he decided drastic action was required and called for back-up in the form of Annette. The only way he could persuade me to take a break from the bath was to invite Annette round to keep me company for a couple of hours, but even then I tried to persuade him to dig out my discarded maternity swimming costume from the attic so that she could sit in the bathroom with me, while I maintained my dignity! I eventually conceded to a two-hour break from my cleansing ritual, giving my body just enough time to regain a slightly more youthful skin condition.

Fortunately, my brief labour started before my skin shrivelled up again on my second bathing stint, and we returned to hospital with a deep sense of satisfaction that I had followed their advice to the nth degree and had kept clean!

Bruce was very supportive during the birth, but did feel a little redundant. His eyes lit up when the midwife gave him a job to do towards the end. He had to press a button when the birth was imminent so that a second midwife could come in. He was so excited by the fact that he could actually do something worth-while that he stopped supporting me as he had been doing for the last three hours. Suddenly all brow-mopping, hand-holding and encouraging words went out of the window as he applied all concentration on the task in hand, and just stared at this red button.

I'll never forget the moment when Max was seconds from arriving, I was in major pain and could tell it was near, when the midwife said, 'Hang on a minute – don't push. Do you mind if a student nurse comes in to watch the birth?' I really couldn't have cared if the whole of the Arsenal first eleven had been there at that point. God knows what the poor girl must have thought, though, because the sight of me must have been enough to put anyone off a career in nursing.

I then had the pleasure of needing an unforgettable set of stitches, and again two more student nurses were invited in to observe. There was quite an audience by now – two midwives, three student nurses, Bruce and, just for good measure, the cleaner stuck her head around the door. Having been determined not to need stirrups for the birth, I was horrified to discover that they had to be used for the stitches. But the elation of giving

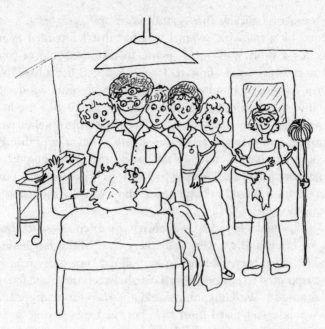

Just for good measure, the cleaner stuck her head around the door

birth must have done strange things to my brain, because as I lay there, legs stretched at nearly a 180-degree angle, with an audience of six and a spotlight up my duff, I really could not give a damn!

It was at this point that I realized I had not used the gas and air properly during the birth. I was given it again to help reduce the pain of the stitches being inserted. I was so relaxed that I actually breathed in deeply and used the gas and air properly for the first time. I suddenly discovered its powers and announced to my audience, 'I'm as high as a kite.' Being teetotal, this was a whole new experience. I think I might try and purchase a little cylinder of the stuff for special occasions!

The reality for me was that living with the stitches for a week after the birth was actually worse than the birth itself. I walked like one of the characters from *Planet of the Apes* and couldn't sit, stand or basically move at all with any great ease. I was advised by a midwife, when I told her that I intended taking Max for a short walk in his pram, to take a couple of pain-killers before I went. True to form, I ignored her advice, and after a couple of hundred yards I was in absolute agony. So much so that Bruce had to go and get the car to take me back home. This agony lasted about a week until the stitches were removed, and then the relief was superb. I never ever thought I would be able to contemplate having sex again, but then I remembered that after having had all four wisdom teeth out I didn't think I would ever eat again, and I was slightly consoled by this thought.

The hospital where Max was born was particularly strict about visiting hours and we were made very clear of this fact before-hand. Partners were allowed to visit all day, but other relatives were restricted to just one hour a day, between three and four in the afternoon. Well, my mum could not grasp this concept at all and was adamant that I must have got the times wrong due to my shrunken brain. She rang the hospital at least ten times during my three-hour labour – the midwives kept coming in and saying, 'Mrs Bettridge, it's your mother on the phone *again*.' They must have been relieved that my labour was short, otherwise they would have been on first-name terms with her! As soon as she found out that Max had been born, she left her home in the West Country and travelled for three hours to see her first grandson. She was horrified when a midwife told her at ten to three that she would not be allowed in for another ten minutes and promptly told the midwife that her daughter had given birth, as if this was going to make any difference when visiting a postnatal ward. It was hardly unusual news for the midwife! After five minutes of coping with an irate little Greek lady bouncing up and down outside the ward and shouting into the intercom, the midwife came and got Bruce to go and pacify her outside until visiting time! I hasten to add at this point, though, that my mum and I are actually very close and I was delighted to see her.

It was such an emotional moment when she gave me a special gift of a ring that had been especially made out of jewellery of sentimental value to our family. As I welled up at this memorable mother–daughter moment, my mother spotted the Arsenal Babygro her newborn grandson was wearing, and once again all hell broke loose!

Annette

* * *

For some strange and naïve reason, I kept thinking that labour would not be that bad. I had heard horror stories about the agony and nasties, but I just thought that these stories were one-offs and that my labour would be OK. It did not help that when I asked any female friend or family member about the pain, they would reassuringly say that it was not too bad. How stupid was I not to read between the lines at these non-descriptive evasive responses from everyone?

I finished work two weeks before my due date. The first week was a novelty, and I had a really good time getting up late, going out for lunch every day, and then having a cosy afternoon nap to make up for the lack of sleep during the night. The second week, I was really impatient. I was fat, hot and I just wanted the baby out. So much so that we had to suffer three false-alarm trips to hospital during that second week!

The first incident was on the Sunday, when I was lying on the sofa watching the Formula One Grand Prix and I stood up quickly to answer the phone. I felt this strange popping sensation followed by a wet feeling. That was enough for me – I ran to the toilet to have a look and was convinced that my waters had broken. So I grabbed my overnight bag, which had been packed nine weeks earlier, and dragged Gavin off to the hospital.

On arrival at the hospital, the midwives were great. They took all the details and performed a water test to confirm the situation.

Unfortunately, the test proved negative and I had to face up to the fact that I had wet myself. They did detect a urine infection and put me straight on antibiotics. So it had not been a complete waste of time. In total, we spent two hours at the hospital before being sent home, dragging my overnight bag behind us. Just to rub salt into my wounds of disappointment, a woman was wheeled past on a trolley and called my name out. It was the Local Yokel from our antenatal classes. She had just given birth and introduced us to her new son. I was so jealous, and as I looked at the little mite I thought bitterly that the poor chap would probably be in his first pair of green wellies before his first birthday! I then had to explain why I was at the hospital, and why I was being sent home. I felt very embarrassed, particularly since I had religiously done my pelvic-floor exercises every morning sitting in the traffic jam to get on to the motorway.

Gavin was very understanding about the incident and kept making kind comments like, 'It was a useful practice run.' But later I found out that he had had a good laugh at work with his friends at my expense over coffee and Danish pastries.

The rest of the week proceeded without incident until the Saturday morning. I was wandering around the local auction-house when I started having contractions. I was highly excited about this, and started measuring the length of time between them, which was approximately ten minutes. I decided to keep quiet and keep going. I lasted until lunchtime, when I shared the news with Gavin. I felt the urge to keep walking around and so we decided to go for a long walk and then phone the hospital when we got back. The more I walked about, the stronger the contractions became and the more excited I became. When Bruce phoned that afternoon to say that Andrea had given birth to Max the night before, I kept thinking, 'Lucky Andrea – it's all over for her, but that'll be me tonight too!'

We phoned the hospital in the evening, and they said to go in for an examination. So out popped the overnight bag again and we trundled off to hospital. On arrival, all the basic checks were done again – blood pressure, pulse and baby heartbeat. I knew the routine by now, and was convinced that I was ready for action, but the internal examination showed that I was only two centimetres dilated, and so it was agreed that I should go home and come back when the contractions were stronger. So back we went, with my bag in tow *again*. As you can imagine, I did not sleep much that night.

On the Sunday, the contractions were coming every five minutes and were stronger and more painful. I held out until the evening and then phoned the hospital. They asked us to come in again, so out came the bag and off we went, only to find out that I was *still* only two centimetres dilated. To top it all, the midwife informed me that this could go on for up to a week – I was not happy. Tired and emotional, we set off home again, Gavin, me and Bertie Bag. Unfortunately, by now I was not the only one who was fed up. Gavin had a grump and informed me that he was not prepared to take me into hospital again on another 'bloody false alarm'. I felt completely sorry for myself. I was in pain, tired and worn down and his lack of sympathy was not helping.

I was so knackered that I managed to get a few hours' sleep that night, but woke up feeling very uncomfortable. Since my last trip to the hospital, I felt as though I still had the midwife's hand up my vagina, and this feeling got gradually worse.

I got up and walked around. It was about two a.m., so I put Ceefax on TV and used the TV clock to measure the time between contractions, which was about four minutes. They were definitely getting stronger now, but I did not dare wake Gavin for fear of it being another 'bloody false alarm'. So I suffered in silence until five o'clock, when I thought the pain was strong enough to warrant waking him up. Gavin then, dragging his heels, took an hour and a half to get ready, and we finally arrived with Bertie at hospital at about seven on the Monday morning. On arrival, all the normal checks were done again – by now, I was so familiar with them I could have done them myself – and guess what? Still only two centimetres dilated! Morale was at an all-time low! I needed a glimmer of hope to spur me on, and there was nothing coming from the midwife. Having seen Gavin's face at this news, they decided to keep me in this time and sent me down to the antenatal ward. By now I was really in pain and could see no end. When I arrived at the antenatal ward at ten o'clock, I found that I had been conned, as they could not administer pain relief there, so I spent the next hour and a half trying to get sent back up to the labour ward.

Eventually, at midday, I was transferred back to the labour ward, where I had pethidine and gas and air. This was another con, as I am sure these are no help at all. They just take your mind off things. By this time I also had my TENS pain-relief machine on at full power, and guess what? I was still only two centimetres dilated. I learnt very quickly that to avoid being sent back down to antenatal you had to insist that you needed the gas and air, so this is what I did. Gavin kept feeding me chocolate for the next few hours to give me energy, and at five-thirty I was officially diagnosed as being in labour. *Yippee!* The time flew past and by nine in the evening I was ready to push, which took everyone by surprise as I am sure they all thought that I had moved in for good.

My waters had to be broken at the last moment, and when I finally had permission to push, I just could not do it. I was so exhausted it took me a good hour to build up the energy, and finally at 11.18 p.m. it happened – out popped Emily in all her glory. The most peculiar bit was when she wriggled with the final push. I could not bear to look in case anything was wrong with her, but Gavin had been running backwards and forwards from my head to my bum giving me a running commentary. And he finally said, 'She's perfect, she's beautiful,' at which point I opened my eyes and they put her in my arms. She was gorgeous!

I did not sleep at all that night, what was left of it. I was on such a high. Gavin was asked to leave as it was so late. And when breakfast arrived the next morning, I ate for England. I have never enjoyed a cup of tea and some Cornflakes so much. I had earned them!

It's funny, but when people ask me now, months later, what my labour was like, I too say, 'Not too bad.' What a hypocrite! Or is it just that I have an extremely poor memory? I bumped into Sarah just one day after giving birth, and even then I managed to say the same to her. But then again, one week before her due date, what else could I say?

The first time I changed Emily's nappy, though, I couldn't help but shed a little tear as I looked down at her and thought, 'You poor thing, one day you will be going through the same experience.'

Sarah

* * *

Labour – how aptly named. I quote a friend when I say that 'That was the hardest day's work I've ever done.' I remember the sheer marvel I felt at how the female body performs at full output as it gives birth to a baby. It's as if your whole body takes over, grasps the task in hand and sees it through to the bitter end, whether that be four hours or twenty-four hours later. The heart's pumping manically, the lungs are filling to their maximum and emptying at varying rates, the stomach forgets that it hasn't eaten for several hours and decides to wait until more important things have finished, the bladder and bowels try desperately to remain in the background but occasionally make themselves known when they really can't hold back any longer, and fortunately the mind stays well out of the way as the bump rules the situation for as long as it takes! Labour is something that makes me feel proud to be a woman and privileged to have experienced childbirth, something which men will never have the benefit of experiencing. It is such a precious thing, which no one will ever be able to take away from you.

On my due date, instead of giving birth to a little bundle of joy, I found myself spending three nights in hospital with high blood pressure. As I was told to rest and keep my feet up, I just sat there in the antenatal ward, watching women arrive, and then the same women depart with their babies. My consultant began talking of inducing me if my blood pressure did not resume a safe level, but I managed to persuade her at last to let me go home to continue resting. How pleased I was to feel my contractions starting naturally, without medical intervention, on the same afternoon I left hospital.

My labour began mildly in the late afternoon of a cold and stormy June day. I wasn't sure at first whether or not they were real contractions or merely strong Braxton Hicks – the sort which can be termed fake contractions. Fortunately, they were real, and as they progressed, I kept pacing around in order to keep them going. If there were two things I was absolutely determined to concentrate on during labour, they were to remain mobile to encourage the effect of gravity, and to breathe consciously through the pain. Can you think of anything more ridiculous than someone advising you to breathe through the pain? But women who have had babies understand exactly what that means – knowing that the pain is only going to last a few seconds, you quickly learn to literally breathe through it to make it more bearable.

Now I am the sort of person who will listen politely to someone's advice, then go and do exactly what I think is best afterwards, and Fiona the midwife's advice on the labour 'bum wiggle' was one such case in point. I was never too sure whether her demonstration of the wiggle was a worthwhile addition to the antenatal class or simply just another opportunity for her to flash her knickers. How wrong I was to be so cynical: the wiggling, or swaying from side to side, was an essential part of my dealing with the first stage of labour. That, coupled with the breathing, was so instinctive and came so naturally that I wonder if we would have bent double and wiggled our backsides in the air if we had never even so much as set foot in an antenatal class. In fact, so essential were these methods of coping with the pain that I did them all the way round the block when I persuaded Tim to accompany me on a midnight walk to ensure my contractions didn't peter out. It was a squally night and I was wrapped in an assortment of clothes that I had grabbed from the wardrobe, including tracksuit bottoms, wellies, Barbour, hat and scarf. Any passer-by would have been excused for thinking we were on our way to a November hunt, rather than taking a first-stage-of-labour stroll round the neighbourhood in late June. Every few hundred yards I had to stop and perform the obligatory bum wiggle, hands on knees, breathing long and deep through the contractions. It was at one of these stops that I told Tim not to feel obliged to stroke me. In fact, I instructed him positively not to touch me whilst I was experiencing a contraction because it would only break my concentration. I already felt that this was going to be a mind-over-matter kind of experience and any interruption would simply hamper progress. So Tim stood loyally beside me each time, hands in pockets, kicking at the stones on the pavement, trying to play the understanding husband but secretly attempting to hide me from passing motorists. I can't blame him, because to anyone watching I would have looked like a straggler from a pub crawl, chucking up in the gutter.

After a hot bath and a quick kip, I decided the pain was sufficient to warrant attaching the TENS machine I had hired two weeks before. It was quite frightening to think that this was no longer a dry run. I was now going to put this piece of machinery to the test. I then spent the next three hours literally pacing the house, punctuating the pacing with wiggles and heavy breathing. It's a wonder we didn't need to re-carpet the stairs and landing afterwards. It surprised me how quickly those three hours went, but I expect it was a combination of concentrating on the contractions and gripping the TENS zapper as if my life depended on it that kept my mind focused. When my contractions were two to three minutes apart and I needed more pain relief, I decided to wake Tim to take me to the hospital. I can honestly say that those few hours by myself gave me the chance to come to terms with what was happening to my body, and I felt very grateful for that.

By the time I got to the hospital, which is only fifteen minutes' drive away, I practically crawled into the delivery suite. We had heard Fiona's description of a woman in labour whom she once came across in the maternity-wing entrance, on her hands and knees, swaying merrily to herself and totally oblivious of anything or anyone around her. At the time I put it down to another old midwives' tale, but I was an action replay of that woman. Fortunately, I was disguised by the cover of darkness, not to mention the Barbour, hat and scarf, but I was oblivious to everything around me whilst concentrating on my contraction. You can imagine how chuffed I was to discover that I was already nine centimetres dilated when they examined me. The pacing about had worked. It would have been worth the expense of re-carpeting the entire house to get news like that!

I was remarkably *compos mentis* throughout the second stage of labour and remember being concerned about how green Tim was looking. I grabbed his hand at one point and said to him, 'Why don't you just go outside for some fresh air? It will do you good.' Contrary to his usual behaviour, he obeyed. He told me afterwards that it was the heat of the room that had made him feel queasy. Of course it was! When he returned, refreshed, he was raring to go. After having told him earlier not to touch me whilst I was going through labour, he was chuffed when I asked him to help out by mopping my forehead with green hospital paper-towels. Pleased with his new role of chief paper-towel attendant, he skilfully obeyed my demands to 'Put it on my forehead', 'Soak the towel again' and 'Take it off.' As the action hotted up, however, Tim's attention was drawn to the lower end of the bed, away from his towel duties. After a particularly large contraction, which involved a manic shaking of my head and a severe 'moo', I was heard to scream at Tim, '*Get the bloody towel off my face!'* My vigorous head-shaking had dislodged the delicately placed, sopping-wet towel, which had crept down across my face until I couldn't see a thing. For some strange reason, the prospect of me actually releasing my grip from the bars of the bed long enough to remove the paper towel myself was way beyond the realms of my imagination. My commanding outburst soon put paid to Tim's display of understanding.

During this second stage of labour, the midwife asked Tim to take the gas-and-air mouth-piece away from me, because I was enjoying the floating sensation so much that I was not concentrating on pushing. Having taken charge of the gas-and-air pump, he then proceeded to warn me each time he saw a contraction coming, by studying the display monitor beside us. With each contraction, he would pass comments such as, 'That wasn't as big as the last one' or '*Cor*, this looks like it's going to be a big one.' All he got in response was a continuous pattern of groans.

For the whole week after Jack was born, I couldn't work out why I had such sore triceps. They had been nowhere near the action, and surely it couldn't be due to picking up a new baby – after all, eight pounds two ounces isn't that heavy. Eventually, I twigged – I had been gripping on to the overhead back bars of the delivery bed with such force throughout the last stages of labour that the sheer exertion had bruised my arm muscles. I wonder if I could request that they put padding around the bars if I have a second baby! My sore arms, and the strange sensation of having had all the stuffing punched out of me, left me feeling like a very tender specimen of a woman, in need of a lot of rest. This was a spectre quite different from the roaring machine I had been just a few hours before.

Lyndsey

* * *

I remember this vividly. I woke at six o'clock on not just any July Saturday morning but *the* Saturday that my baby was due, forty weeks to the day, according to my dates. 'Damn,' I thought, 'I need to go to the loo,' an early-morning habit that I was getting fed up with. When I went to the toilet I saw a small, dark-brown bloodstain on my pants which I examined closely. No, there was no mucus plug, so I returned to bed in slight disbelief that this could be *it*. I then experienced period-type pains in my groin, but as I had been having these on and off over the last couple of days, I tried to close my eyes and get some sleep. No such luck. I became obsessed with the frequency of these dull aches and by seven o'clock I nudged Tim to say that I may be in labour. As I didn't seem to be screaming the house down or flooding the bed, Tim grunted that it was too early in the morning to get excited and promptly rolled back over to get some more sleep.

At ten o'clock I was ringing Hilary to explain that perhaps it would be best if I did not attend the antenatal exercise class, as I thought I was in labour. 'What do you mean, you *think* you are in labour – surely you must know?' Hilary asked gruffly. In fact, she was a bit put out, as she didn't want to be the last one out of our group left to drop. The two of us had been getting more paranoid and nervous as each new baby arrived, and our battle of the babies had commenced. Although Hilary was due after me, there was always the chance that if I were late and she were early she could pip me at the post. 'Are you sure this isn't just an excuse to get out of the exercise class, Lyndsey?' She was still in denial mode, but hearing the groan as another dull ache made its presence felt, she conceded that perhaps pelvic thrusts should be exchanged for a warm bath and some relaxation tapes.

I was becoming more convinced that this was probably labour, but I had been expecting strong contractions which would start from the top of my stomach, and not these dull aches low down in my groin. By eleven o'clock we decided to ring the hospital to warn them of an impending arrival, and I was encouraged to stay at home for as long as possible.

It was a lovely hot summer day and Tim got the sun-loungers out of the garage, stripped off, jumped on to a lounger, closed his eyes and started to sunbathe. Meanwhile, my contractions had intensified, and remembering Sarah's advice to keep moving, I headed off for the field behind our back garden and breathed my way around it. By one o'clock I had stuck the TENS machine on and marched back out to the field, which was becoming too small for my needs. I felt like David Bellamy setting out on a new exploration with hiking boots and a copy of an Ordnance Survey map tucked under my arm. Anything to take my mind off the contractions. Should I take the mobile phone, I wondered,

No, I'm fine here, thanks

in case I got to the top of the field and found myself at the point of no return? Tim, meanwhile, applied another splash of suntan oil and continued to enjoy the rays. When I asked if he would care to join me for a lap of the field or beyond, he answered, 'No, I'm fine here, thanks.' I could have hit him.

At two o'clock we phoned the hospital again, but it was difficult to time the contractions. They were either two to three minutes apart and then only thirty seconds in duration and bearable, or they were five to six minutes apart, then lasted at least a minute and were hell. Again I was told to hang on for as long as possible, but by five o'clock I was screaming that I needed a bit more than an electrical impulse and a stomp around the field – *I needed drugs!*

We had heard in the press that a baby boom was forecast for that summer, such that the local hospital might not have space to cope with the new arrivals. The other three had had their babies on relatively quiet days, but it turned out that one of the recurring nightmares that I had had as the birth had drawn nearer was now a reality. It seems the whole world and their dog were having their babies that afternoon, and I was told that all the delivery suites were occupied. Oh God, I groaned! What did that mean for me? I could see it now – I was going to end up having my baby in the corridor, or worse still in the sluice room. The last thing I wanted to do was bear down on the floor, and an immediate thought was that I hadn't done enough leg exercises for a squatting birth. What was going to be my alternative? A dash to another hospital twenty miles away? Perhaps I could get one of Andrea's colleagues to give me a blue-light escort all the way. I never thought I would be relieved to be shown to what appeared to be a broom cupboard which housed all the extinct equipment. This was an improvement on the corridor, as at least it did have a bed in it, but I wondered if it was an omen as to how the birth was going to go.

A long half-hour later, the midwife came to examine me and I waited eagerly for her findings. Bearing in mind that this had all started twelve hours previously, I was expecting her to announce that I was at least six or seven centimetres dilated. Of course, as every mother-to-be should know, ten centimetres is the jackpot. Once you hit that, all the lights start flashing and you can 'Go, go, go, push, push, push.' Hilary and I had heard how Sarah had been nine centimetres dilated on her arrival at the hospital, and I had various friends who had proudly announced they had been either six, seven or eight centimetres. It was becoming an obsession, so when the midwife proclaimed that I was three centimetres, my jaw fell and you could have knocked me over with a feather. 'Three centimetres! *Three measly centimetres! Is that all?*' I shouted. This was going to be a long night, as the usual rule-of-thumb is an hour for every centimetre dilated. It took no Einstein to work out that I had at least another seven hours to go, and so we were left for four hours to amuse ourselves. I remember looking out of the window at the passers-by on the street and saying to Tim that I wished I could be out there with them on this lovely summer evening, rather than cooped up with a bunch of rusty old machinery. He calmed me down by saying that it would soon be over and he would then treat me to a pint of lager, which, at that moment, seemed like heaven.

At one of the foetal checks, Tim asked the midwife if she believed in any of the old wives' tales about whether I was carrying a boy or a girl. She said the only one she stood by was the heartbeat, which we could hear at that time via the monitor, and that it was slower for a girl than a boy. She guessed that we were soon to have a little girl, but then went on to say that although she was usually right, she had got it wrong for her own kids, so we were back to square one. Two days previously Tim had gone shopping for some pictures for our baby's nursery. He had been convinced that, as he had longed for a girl, we were bound to have a boy, so accordingly he had bought a couple of pictures of Victorian-style teddies with a train, a car and a boat. Just the thing for a little Thomas or Peter, but a bit doubtful for a Lucy or a Bethan. Mind you, Tim was adamant that, whatever the sex, our child would be playing rugby for Wales.

Meanwhile, I was still pacing the room and wishing this baby would arrive. I didn't like the gas and air as it made me feel sick, so I asked for an epidural or pethidine. Eventually, the midwife relented and gave me some pethidine, which relaxed me a bit, but I did not quite manage to snooze between contractions as the midwife had suggested. Tim must have also asked for a shot, because when I glanced at him from my sleepy haze at about one in the morning, there he was having a doze. Bless him, all that waiting must have worn him out, or perhaps it was all that sun!

My waters were eventually broken, and after three more hours, another shot of pethidine and a lot of huffing and puffing, the midwife decided it may be time to help move nature further along. She left the delivery suite, which I had been transferred to at last, to collect the necessary material, and it seemed that as soon as the door had closed I felt an enormous urge to push. I shouted to Tim to find someone and *quickly*, but perhaps I should have been more precise, as the best he could do was come back with someone who looked like a cleaner – and by the look on her face and her hasty retreat, she certainly did not know how to deliver a baby. This is it, I thought. Tim was going to have to roll up his sleeves and deliver this child himself. His tanned face was looking remarkably white at this point. He disappeared out to the corridor again to track down some help – neither of us had thought to press the button by the bed – and this time he returned with not one but two midwives. The cavalry had arrived, and twenty minutes later a little baby was delivered on to my stomach. I looked down to see the slippery bundle and the first thing that struck me was the size of its hands. It seemed all fingers and thumbs, and a quick count revealed that there were six fingers on the hand that I could see. Rather than go into a fit of panic or hysteria, I remember thinking to myself, 'Ah, bless, this baby may have six fingers, but so what? I don't care – it's just a relief to see it out in one piece.' It was a strange reaction, after all the worry which had haunted me from the day I found out I was pregnant as to whether or not there would be any problems such as deformities. I had imagined that I would have crumbled into pieces at even the slightest abnormality, rather than sit there with a smirk on my face, proud that the baby had an extra digit. As it turned out, the midwife's counting was a tad more accurate than mine, and she pronounced that everything was fine, fingers and toes included, but did we not want to know the sex? I had put on my birth plan that we wanted to determine the sex of the baby ourselves and so the midwife had hung back, waiting for us to investigate further. I had been so preoccupied with the hands, and Tim was still in a state of shock from what he had just witnessed, that neither of us had had the idea to check to see whether we had a boy or a girl. We both took a cautious look and beamed that yes, it was a girl. 'And do you have a name for your daughter?' the midwife asked. We both looked at each other, smiled and simultaneously announced, 'Bethan.'

Hilary

***

My lasting memory of labour is sitting through the night watching video after video of series one and two of *Friends*. I will never know if I could have slept through those early contractions, because the excitement of labour starting, combined with my complete love of *Friends*, meant that there was absolutely no way I was going to go to sleep. David, however, went for the sensible option of banging in a good few hours' kip before the fun started. I suppose the fact that he delivers either piglets or lambs almost on a daily basis was partly responsible for his cool, calm exterior, which came as no surprise to me. Having said that, I have to admit that even I was surprised at just how calm he was when I did wake him. I decided to leave his alarm call to the last possible moment, just so I could enjoy watching his reaction to my request for a lift to the hospital. So at six o'clock, I very calmly, quietly and gently shook him awake and suggested that when he was ready he ought to get dressed, as my contractions were three minutes apart. For some reason, I had expected to see him leap into action, but when he had not appeared in the lounge ten minutes later, I returned to find him sound asleep! It turned out that he thought I'd actually meant it when I'd asked him to get ready 'in his own time'. Unbelievable! If he was that calm with our first child, I dread to think what he will be like by number four – I will probably have to drive myself to hospital.

I have a complete aversion to hospitals, to put it mildly, so I really did want to leave my admission to the last possible minute. What I did not realize was that contractions can be quite frequent but not actually doing much. I thought I really was in the throes of labour when we went to hospital, but retrospectively it is clear this must have been wishful thinking! When I got to hospital, I was asked to go to the toilet and provide a urine sample. It looked as though a massacre had taken place in the toilet, which had clearly not been cleaned since the previous lady had visited it after giving birth to her child. I realized that I still had a long way to go before my baby arrived when I found myself wearing a pair of rubber gloves, on my hands and knees, cloth and cream cleaner in hand, scrubbing the hospital toilet! Once the task was done, I decided that I might as well return home until things heated up a bit. The midwives were somewhat surprised, but secretly I think they were grateful to free up a bed and get rid of this overkeen first-time mum. However, they could not have been as grateful as the cleaner, who must have been thrilled to discover that the toilet fairy had been in to do her job!

David remained cool, calm and casual all day, and even found my contraction-coping mechanism of wriggling my backside at a ninety-degree angle a great source of entertainment. Every time I bent forward and started to sway my hips, he thought it extremely witty to shout, 'Whey hey!' as he pelvic-thrusted behind me. The first couple of times he did this, I had to admit that I did laugh, but as the contractions progressed I had a serious sense-of-humour failure. During one particularly powerful contraction I felt him come up behind me, and I thought he was up to his usual antics. I opted for the quickest way I could think of to get rid of him, and booted him in the shins. He was livid. It turned out that the poor chap was actually coming up behind me to massage my back and was not whey-heying at all! '*You are not a mule,*' he shouted. '*There is no need to behave like one.*' So that told me! It was only afterwards that it struck me that one little kick in the shins, compared with the hours and hours of labour I was going through, was really a minor discomfort he could and should have tolerated.

Before returning to hospital, I decided to go for the statutory bath so highly recommended by the midwives. By this time, though, I was having a love affair with my TENS machine, which I was extremely reluctant to give up. I waited until the last possible moment, and as I stepped into the bath I handed the controls to David and asked him to switch it off and remove the pads. The mule incident suddenly faded into insignificance, as he accidentally (so he says) whacked the TENS machine up to full throttle instead of off, and I nearly hit the ceiling! It was as though someone had hit the 'go' button on the electric chair. I swear that if my TENS machine had been attached to the mains, the whole town's lights would have dimmed briefly, with the amount of power that was sent through my back! 'Shall we call it evens?' said David, with a huge grin on his face, once I had settled into my lovely bubbly bath. It is a good job I could not move at that point, or I would have been removing certain parts of his anatomy, essential for parenthood, and been wearing them for earrings!

On top of my dislike for hospitals, I also did not want to return too quickly due to my slightly unconventional choice of birthing music. My mother had very kindly bought me a compact disc of pan-pipe music to help me relax, but in the weeks leading up to my due date I had played this and come to the conclusion that it would drive me absolutely nuts if I was in any pain. I decided, therefore, to opt for Meat Loaf's 'Bat Out of Hell', an altogether far more apt choice, I felt. I found this absolutely brilliant for getting the breathing right in the final stages of labour. I am just not sure if the lady giving birth in the next room appreciated it quite as much. It was a case of:

> *'Sirens are screaming and the fires are howling way down in the valley tonight.'*
> Big breath in.
> *'There's a man in the shadow with a gun in his eye and a blade shining oh so bright.'*
> Big breath in.
> *'There's evil in the air and thunder in the sky and the killer's on the bloodshot street.'*
> Big breath in.
> *'Way down in the tunnel where the deadly are rising, you know I swear I saw a young boy down in the gutter he was starting to foam in the heat.'*
> Big breath in.
> *'And like a bat out of hell . . .'*

And so it went on. The timing and the length of the lines is so spot on for labour breathing, I think Meat Loaf should market this idea! Much to David's relief, I knew all the words, so we did not need the actual tape playing. He just elbowed me whenever a midwife walked in to get me to shut up when we were in company. I think he would have been much happier with the pan pipes, poor bloke.

My final memory of labour is the mooing. Whenever you see a film with someone giving birth, they always seem to moo like a cow during their contractions. Being a farmer, this has always been a great source of amusement for David, who spent my whole pregnancy winding me up by saying, 'Are you going to moo like a cow?' as he lay on our bed with his legs in the air shouting, '*Moooo, moooo!*' (and *he* was going to be the father!). Well, by the very end of my labour, even 'Bat out of Hell' was not helping, and much to my horror I found I was doing a full-blown cow impression into my Entonox mouth-piece. Every time I caught David's eye, I could see straight into his thoughts and desperately tried denying my animal impressions between contractions.

Well, despite the mooing, singing, kicking and electric-shock treatment, Molly arrived safe and sound, and although at the time I remember thinking that the whole experience was horrendous and something I would never do again, here I am four months down the line, planning to have many, many more mooing experiences, and the Bat Out of Hell turned out to be my Baby Out of Heaven!

Owning a Baby

Nobody can really give you any idea of what it is going to be like actually to *own* (for want of a better word) a baby. The gap between being a pregnant woman and being a mother is *so* huge, it makes the Grand Canyon look like a crack in the pavement. Yet, no matter how well prepared you think you are, with all the equipment going, nursery decorated and every book on the market purchased and read, you still have to leap that gap and make the transition from one person to two with no emotional warning or understanding of what it can possibly feel like.

This chapter will look at some of our fears, and how we handled and overcame them. The full-time care of a newborn child is a responsibility like no other, and it is hard to believe that every day thousands of women, with absolutely no previous experience, are released into the community, each with the sole responsibility of caring for a helpless new person.

Imagine if they took the same approach to employing an airline pilot. Picture the interview scene: 'So you've never flown a plane before then, but you have read a couple of books and been to a few classes. Great, you sound perfect for the job, you can start straight away. Off you go. There's a Boeing 747 out there on the runway. Could you just whizz the four hundred passengers on board to Singapore for us? We've left a map on the dashboard for you, so we think you'll be all right. See you later!'

It's unbelievable really, isn't it? But we all muddle through, and these babies seem to be pretty resilient. Here goes with some of the fears and mistakes we made on our 'first flights'. Luckily none of us has crashed and burned to date!

Andrea

* * *

From the moment Max arrived, it was as though a huge weight had been placed on our shoulders, which would not be lifted for another eighteen years or so. That is, if it is ever lifted at all, because I am sure as parents we will feel responsible for ever. It was due to this parental sense of responsibility that Max was not born two or three years earlier. I was very keen and broody, but Bruce kept saying that he did not feel grown up enough and, what's more, he did not want to give up his carefree days so soon. He explained that he wanted us to do all of the irresponsible things first to get them out of our system before we started a family. So we went on holidays together, I went on wild football tournaments and we generally had a good time. I even went on one football tournament when I was thirty-eight weeks pregnant, much to Bruce's disgust. I was secretly hoping that the excitement might persuade Max to arrive early – although not too early, as the tournament was in Essex, and I did not want him to be labelled an Essex lad.

I am not exactly sure when the responsibility side of things really hit us, but it was either during the car journey home from the hospital, or in the first half-hour at home, when we both sat staring at Max as he slept in his car seat in our lounge. We were suddenly slapped in the face with the cold reality that he was totally dependent on us, God help him, and that there was no turning back. When I look back now, those first three or four days were unreal. Bruce and I did not really have a clue what we were doing, and I used to save up pages and pages of questions to ask the midwife when she visited me each day.

I have to laugh now when I remember the black-poo incident. Had I paid a bit more attention in the antenatal classes or even read a book or two, I would have known that a newborn baby's first few poos are a sort of black colour due to the meconium. Bruce and I tackled Max's first nappy together, and we thought he was seriously ill when we saw the black tar-like substance. We were just about to make total fools of ourselves by ringing the hospital when Annette rang. She reassured us that it was totally normal – and she had not even given birth yet! We soon settled into a little routine, and over the first few days, as I watched various visitors clumsily clutching my newborn, I realized that I was rapidly becoming an expert. Well, at least I had mastered the skill of clutching with confidence.

Dressing Max, however, was a different matter. We got the hang of Babygros, but anything more complicated, involving zips or buttons, and we were useless. Needless to say, Max managed to spend the first month of his life alternating between the home- and away-strip Arsenal Babygro. On the first occasion that I did brave attempting some alternative attire, Bruce was livid to discover his son in what he termed a sailor's outfit. It did slightly resemble a dress, I must admit, and as Bruce undressed Max that night for his bath he said, 'Don't *ever* put my son in a dress again – I can't handle these buttons.' I was tempted to try Max in a dress without buttons on another occasion, just to test whether it was the dress or the buttons that his father objected to. What I didn't dare tell him was that the sailor's outfit was in fact a present from his mother.

It took about a fortnight before I was brave enough to venture out with Max on my own. I had heard stories from Annette about how she had met Sarah and Lyndsey for lunch at a local wine bar, with their babies, and I was horrified. I couldn't imagine taking Max out with me at all, let alone for lunch at this early stage. What if he woke up, cried, wanted feeding or, worse still, a nappy change? Obviously these fears wore off with time, but I was very impressed with the others' bravery so soon after the birth of their babies.

My first outing with Max turned out to be an absolute disaster. It had rained non-stop for about two weeks and I was desperate to take him for a walk in his pram. One Sunday afternoon my football team were training on a pitch about an hour's walk from home, so I agreed to stroll up there to show off my new pride and joy. It was a hot and humid summer's day, so I dressed him in cute little matching shorts and T-shirt, no zips or buttons involved, gave him a bottle of milk and then placed him in the pram. As I proudly ambled off, I was totally oblivious to the fact that I was in fact roasting my son alive in the midday sun! I did manage to put the sunshade up, but they are only really any good if you go in exactly the same direction all the time without turning corners. Poor Max must have been cursing as his milk curdled and churned around in his tiny little tummy as we went over the rough canal tow-path. After about half a mile, it was all too much for him and he threw up everywhere. Not just a little puke, but a major *Exorcist*-style one. I picked him up and he was boiling hot, all of his clothes were soaked with sweat, not to mention vomit, and he was not just crying but screaming incon- solably. I was distraught, but somehow Bruce must have had a sixth sense that something was wrong because as I stood there howling in unison with Max, he appeared from nowhere, bundled us all into the car, ignoring the need for car seats, and whisked us back to the safe haven of home. I remembered Flash Your Knickers Fiona giving advice in an antenatal class about 'washing baby down with a cool flannel' if they had a tempera- ture, and we promptly did this. Within five minutes Max was fine, but I felt extremely guilty about the whole event. I relayed the story to our health visitor later, and she cheered me up by telling me of a similar experience she had had herself with her own daughter. I was consoled by the fact that even health professionals can be inadequate parents! The whole incident made me realize just how much I now had to put Max and his needs first. For the rest of the summer, Max was restricted to late-afternoon strolls only – covered like a cross-channel swimmer with factor-fifty suntan lotion. We decided to protect his delicate skin from the midday sun by staying home to watch *Neighbours*.

Before Max was born, I was determined not to become one of those parents who bored everyone to death by constantly waffling on and on about their new baby. It is not that I object to hearing other people's stories – in fact, I quite enjoy them – but I wanted to be able to hold conversations about other matters too. This objective has proved to be much harder than I thought. It is not just the talking about our babies but the subjects we have discussed that have amazed me.

My very saddest conversation, I have to admit, took place whilst I was visiting a friend in Yorkshire. Max had a slight tummy upset and I used up his whole supply of nappies before the end of our visit. I went out to the village stores but was not able to purchase my usual brand of nappies. When I returned with an alternative supply, I mentioned this to my friend and we then had a very long and detailed chat about the pros and cons of the different brands. I tell you, we could have written a consumer survey by the time we had finished! There I was, visiting a mate I hadn't seen for many months, with lots of exciting news to tell her, and what did we talk about? Nappies! I am not holding my breath for my next invitation – I probably bored her so much that she could not wait to get rid of us.

I do believe, however, that things may change when I return to work. I say this because I have noticed a distinct change in Annette's conversations since she went back. I can tell that she spends her time with adults again because our conversations have a more varied style. We still discuss Emily and Max, but not in such a detailed fashion. So when I go back to work, I will once again be able to bore people with details of my latest arrest, rather than of Max's latest nappies.

Bruce and I were determined that Max would not drastically change our lifestyle – that we would still do things and go places, and Max would just come along with us. He would fit into our lives and come out on adventures rather than confining us to the house never to go anywhere again. So far, he has been to the local pub on more than one occasion, he has visited Highbury twice, and has even been on a day trip to France with Annette and Emily. He has also sat happily watching me play tennis and football and, all being well, he is due to travel to America with me in two months' time to visit relatives, so I think he is fitting in with us quite well.

Max is a huge responsibility, but we both agree that he is totally worth the extra burden on our shoulders, and we would not know what to do if it was suddenly lifted. Bruce has had to travel out of the country on more than one occasion on business, and he says that he thinks of us both all of the time and can't wait to get home to see if Max still recognizes him. Not only wouldn't we want the burden to be lifted, but if I get my way, it will be doubled in another couple of years!

Hilary

* * *

When I was nineteen, I did a nannying job for just three months, and I have never hated anything as much in my life. I was looking after an eight-month-old and an eighteen-month-old, from 8.30 a.m. until 7.30 p.m., five days a week. I felt sick every morning at the prospect of yet another day in the company of infants only, and although they were very well behaved, I counted down every minute of every day because I found caring for such young children completely boring.

Having set the scene, you can imagine therefore just how unenamoured I was at the prospect of having a baby of my very own. This was going to be twenty-four hours a day, seven days a week. I was petrified. I was sick throughout my pregnancy, but this was quite possibly due to nerves and not morning sickness at all! I couldn't bear to look at children for fear of a panic attack coming over me at the prospect of taking full responsibility for my pending arrival.

Most people seem to long for their baby's arrival, but despite my chronic water retention and hideously expanding body, I have to say that I was perfectly happy staying pregnant. As long as the baby was on the inside, I knew it was safe, warm and moving. I didn't have to worry about babysitters, cot death, screaming or feeding, yet I still felt as though I had joined the privileged band of mums. If it hadn't been for the rest of the girlies giving birth before me, I reckon I would have been perfectly happy with, at the very least, the gestation period of an elephant – after all, I looked like one!

As my due date approached and the impending arrival began to seem a reality, the panic really set in, and was made worse by every purchase of essential equipment, such as nappies and Babygros. I was kept awake at night by constant questions in my head. Would I know what to do with the baby? How often do you change a nappy? How do you make a cot up with sheets and blankets? How many blankets would the baby need? What lotions and potions should you use on it and where? The Bounty packs of freebies given out at antenatal class seemed to be full of little nick-nacks which I hadn't got a clue how to use, and I am a nurse! When Lyndsey called in to see me and said that she had bumped into Annette in the chemist's getting something to give her new baby for colic, that just finished me off completely. How did Annette know her baby had colic? What is colic, anyway? At this point, I decided that the only way I was going to survive the last few weeks of pregnancy without my brain exploding from overload was to take the ostrich's head-in-the-sand approach to life until the contractions started.

When Molly did eventually arrive, I think David and I went into total shock. Everyone had told us how emotional that moment is, and that even the hardest of men are reduced to tears. Well neither of us came close to tears, and I am usually a complete wussie – I'll even blub at a wedding on *Eastenders*. We were completely gobsmacked to discover that it actually was a baby that came out! I am not entirely sure what we thought it was going to be, but David had always said that it was all wind and water, so maybe he would have been happy with just a huge fart after all that pushing. We certainly were not mesmerized by the magic of the moment, and made no declarations about the beauty of our newborn. Having seen so many people, blinded by love for their baby, tell everyone how beautiful their child was, when in reality it bore an uncanny resemblance to ET, I was determined not to do the same. When the midwife handed me my baby for the first time, my first words were, 'Bless her, she looks like a cross between Frank Bruno and a character from *Cocoon*.' David was horrified, and refused to let me speak to anyone on the phone until I promised to say she looked lovely.

The smack-in-the-face reality of owning a baby hit David first, when he was asked to 'dress baby' while I had a shower. The poor chap was just left to it, with a ten-minute-old squirming, squealing dot who certainly did not want to lower her knees away from the safety of her own stomach. I returned all refreshed to find a sweaty David discovering that well-known Babygro phenomenon of the spare press-stud. It is a bit like that last teaspoon in the washing-up bowl – no matter how many times you swill your hands around to check the bowl, when you tip the water out there is always one spoon left. With Babygros, no matter where you start the popping process, be it the neck, crotch or leg, when you get to the end you always seem to have that one spare stud, or worse still, two studs but both either 'innies' or 'outies'. I swear they stick a spare one on during the manufacturing process, simply to confuse new parents.

Despite being completely shell-shocked by our new arrival and not even knowing how to do the basics such as change a nappy, my fear of hospitals still got the better of me and we ended up doing a midnight flit when the minimum stay-time was up. Most parents calmly get their baby into its going-home clothes, taking photos as they get into the car and are waved off by the midwife. Not us, we were sneaking out past sleeping mums at 11.45 p.m. with a nervous midwife saying, 'Are you *sure* you don't want to stay until the morning?' Worse still, when we arrived home, we had to make a nursery before we could go to bed. We had bought all the gear but, being a complete pessimist, I had refused to unwrap anything until the baby arrived. So there we were at one in the morning, taking the plastic off the changing mat and cot mattress in order to have a bash at our first nappy change and to make up a bed for the poor little mite.

This may have been an unorthodox start to parenthood, but it is amazing how quickly you get the hang of things when you are thrown in at the deep end, or should I say jump in at the deep end, without any armbands and after only taking theory rather than practical swimming lessons! Two days later I felt almost confident, and after a week I felt like a true professional. I even got the hang of maintaining my favoured eight hours' sleep at night by latching Molly on to my boob in bed and leaving her to it. At one point I fell asleep while she was feeding and woke up four hours later to find her still feeding. I will never know if she ever actually let go at all, or whether she just hung on all night for fear of not being offered a second innings.

I was so proud of the ease with which I seemed to have fallen into motherhood that I became quite blasé about the whole thing. When Molly was a week old, David and I took her shopping. I adeptly removed the car seat Molly was strapped into and walked casually on. As David joined me, he calmly piped up, 'Do you think that is the best angle to carry her at?' When I looked down, I discovered that in my bid to show off how fast I could whip the car seat in and out, I had not clicked the handle into the upright position. To my horror, I was merrily striding out with an upside-down car seat, and my precious new baby, held in only by her straps, was dangling underneath in the free-falling-parachutist position!

Somehow she has managed to survive my dippy clumsy failings so far, but the next hurdle she will have to leap is the discovery that everything in life is not sung. Before having a baby, I was very self-conscious of my inability to talk to a baby in

Do you think that is the best angle to carry her at?

'coochie-coo' language, so when Molly came along I found it easier to sing everything to her rather than talk like a complete fool. Heaven knows why I was less self-conscious about this because, believe me, I am no Ella Fitzgerald. I am to singing what Pavarotti is to dieting. Despite this, I drone on regardless, making up dodgy lyrics to dreadful tunes. If my singing voice does not cause Molly severe psychological damage then my lyrics will certainly turn her into an egotist. Every made-up song is about her, and every nursery rhyme has been re-worked to include her name. It is no longer Mary with that little lamb, and as for Lavender's Blue Dilly Dilly, well Dilly has gone right out the window! When Molly starts nursery school, she is going to be devastated to discover that all these songs are not about her, after all!

Well, four months into motherhood and I still wake up in total shock that I really am a mum, with a baby of my very own.

And more to the point, despite my blunders, I am even doing a convincing job of being a competent mother!

Sarah

* * *

Perhaps this is not a good time to sit down to begin this chapter, in view of the fact that I have just spent all afternoon pacing around the flat in Spain trying to calm my whinging baby. No, that's not strictly true. He hasn't taken up the *whole* afternoon. I have also managed to *half* wash up, *half* hang up a whites wash – or, more specifically, a bibs-and-vests wash – and also boil the kettle twice in the vain hope of making myself a cup of tea. It is now five-thirty and I am sitting down to my first cup of tea of the day, having just got Jack off to sleep. Bliss!

I must stress that at the ripe old age of five months, Jack is not generally a grumpy baby, but today he has been particularly bad. A bad bout of teething, combined with sicking up a lunch of 'Pollo con Arroz' (which, incidentally, is nothing more special than chicken and rice), plus the inevitable accumulated tiredness, resulted in an acute case of bloody-minded baby syndrome – 'Don't you dare put me down in my playnest, or under my baby gym, and certainly not in my rocker. I'm pissed off and want to whimper in your ear for as long as it takes for this mood to pass.' From experience, this syndrome cannot be remedied by shutting the offending baby in another room to let him scream himself to sleep, despite what mothers-in-law tell you. I only lasted fifteen minutes this afternoon and then gave in. At home in the UK I will often leave Jack to cry himself to sleep, as long as he's not in too much of a state, but in the Spanish flat I'm very conscious of our poor neighbours. We can hear their television next door, so I'm sure as hell that they can hear Jack's screams echoing around our sparsely furnished flat.

Sleep deprivation is a part of owning a baby that no one, not even mothers, midwives or experienced friends, can fully prepare you for. Speaking as someone who was once nicknamed by her husband 'the original bed bug', I found getting up at all times of the day and night to feed Jack a real trial. A newborn baby just does not distinguish between light time and dark time, and as its mother your days and nights all roll into one. I remember the time the visiting midwife weighed Jack after ten days and was concerned that he hadn't regained his birth weight. When she advised me to try feeding every three hours instead of the handy four that I was trying to get him accustomed to, I could have nutted her. Did she not realize how much less sleep that would mean me getting during the night? The situation was, of course, aggravated by the fact that Tim, unlike all the other new fathers in this book, did not just sleep in another room, but in another country! As such, he was only able to share in these nocturnal disturbances at weekends. This zombie-like state does not last for ever, fortunately, and if only someone had convinced me of that at the start, it would have made those first couple of months a lot more bearable.

Before Jack was born, Tim and I made a pact that the arrival of a baby would not transform us into baby bores or, even worse, housebound hermits. We even said to our closest friends, 'You have full permission to stop us short if we so much as verge on boring you with baby talk.' So far, we haven't had any such comment. That's either because our friends have decided we are beyond help, or because they are all getting pregnant now themselves, so we are all as boring as each other, or, as I would hope, because we have successfully achieved our aim. Right from day one, we were determined to live according to the principle that the baby comes to live with you, not the other way round. So less than forty-eight hours after Jack's birth, with me still bandy-legged from the birthing experience, Tim and I took Jack for his first pub lunch. Admittedly, our ploughmen's lunches were heavily interrupted by constant essential baby-checks – nappy content, temperature, vomit, winding, etc. It

was extremely stressful on the digestive system, but we had done
it! His next big trip was at two weeks old, when we went away
for the weekend to the wedding of a good friend. Thankfully,
Jack slept peacefully throughout most of the proceedings. This
was very fortunate, considering the minimal emphasis I had put
on preparing for my baby's weekend away, compared to my
preoccupation with ensuring that my wedding outfit made me
look more elegant than an elephant. If anyone had asked me
when my baby was due, I would have been absolutely devastated.

I think Tim was determined to make the adage 'We don't let
our baby rule our lives' a personal motto. This was undoubtedly
made easier for him as he was not spending *all* day and *all* night
with Jack in those first precious weeks. He took his motto so
seriously that when Jack was a sprightly three weeks old, Tim
suggested that we leave him asleep in his pram in the garden for
half an hour while we went shopping. Gut instinct was telling
me that this was a daft idea, but I had real difficulty explaining to
my husband that a baby so young should not be left alone outside
in a pram whilst its our-baby-hasn't-changed-our-lives parents
did their Saturday shop as usual. With hindsight, I realize there
should have been absolutely no dithering on my part. I'm perfectly happy leaving Jack with a responsible babysitter, but the
thought of leaving him on his own is simply not worth contemplating. Moments like this and others – for example, leaving Jack
to cry himself hoarse when he was only two weeks old, to teach
him not to cry for attention – coupled with more major conflicts
in opinion, such as Tim wanting to leave Jack to sleep on his
front, 'Because he sleeps for longer that way,' served to make our
first couple of months as parents extremely stressful. Remnants of
Tim's tough army training were a little too evident for me to
handle, and I feared for how we would ever reach agreement on
later fundamental issues such as schooling and girlfriends!

With time, however, and with a bit more understanding on
both sides, we are reaching a more harmonious stage. Tim is less
demanding during the weekends he is at home, and I am trying

to be more accommodating of his desire to be more involved. This is one reason why I think it was a good idea for Jack and me to spend more time with Tim in Spain.

Since we have been out in Spain, we have already spent several days away in France and in the Spanish Pyrenees. To our relief, we have discovered that basically, wherever sterilizer, bottles and milk go, so will Jack. Despite our frequent jokes with hoteliers that we are moving in, when they stare aghast at the amount of luggage we arrive with for one night, we are pleased with how little we have managed to get the baby bulk reduced to. This is a knack I will obviously have to perfect when it comes to shuttling regularly between Bilbao and Heathrow.

We now use a baby rucksack to enable us to get out and about and do the walking we were so used to doing before. I believe they recommend using them from six months onwards, but Jack quickly grew accustomed to his from the tender age of four months. We had been using the front-carrying sling up until then, but when Jack hit sixteen pounds I felt as though I looked just like an orang-utan as I strode out. All I needed was for someone to paint my bum red and I would have been in danger of being banged up in Whipsnade Zoo! When choosing the backpack, Tim and I spent a good half-hour battling over our contrasting criteria of whether or not it felt comfortable enough on Tim's back and whether or not I liked the colours. Once our choice was narrowed to two, we decided that it would probably be a good idea to try Jack inside them to see if a third criteria of baby comfort might also be worth considering. Unfortunately, it was not long since his last feed, and this trying-out session gave Jack an opportunity to honk on the one he liked best. We felt obliged to purchase the soiled rucksack, which definitely put Jack in my good books, as it was fractionally less comfortable but certainly more attractive. Tim looks forward to the day when Jack can simply say, 'I prefer this one, Dad!'

It must be with abject horror that every mother-to-be sees herself descending into baby talk. Before Jack was born, I secretly believed that my baby would be different, and would be one of those modern, intellectual babies who only react to stimuli such as classical music and foreign languages. However, I soon woke up to reality and, before I knew it, I was competing with other mothers to pull the most contorted face and speak in the most high-pitched voice possible. It is sad but true that those exaggerated facial expressions do in fact get the best responses from a baby. Jack squeals loudest when you give him the biggest grin you can muster and then bury your head in his stomach, blowing a raspberry at the same time. Tim has complained of getting a headache when he has spent more time than usual contorting his face unnaturally and speaking at a higher pitch than he does at work. I haven't heard of baby talk causing brain injury, but if it were possible I would be a prime candidate. I have even found myself cooing at Jack whilst out shopping – however, I soon stop in my tracks, as the memory of how I used to despise women who acted like complete morons over babies in prams comes flooding back. I'm not sure if it is going to be a blessing or a curse that I will be able to coo away to my heart's content when I'm in Spain, because no one will understand a word I'm saying!

It is strange that, having got the owning-a-baby bit sussed in the UK, I now have a whole new learning curve to go through, transferring to the Spanish way of doing things. My phrase book gets me happily around the food markets, but would it be adequate to converse with a doctor, should Jack become ill, for example? I certainly don't think it has a translation for words close to an English mother's heart such as Bickipegs and Calpol! The Spanish, however, seem to be utterly fascinated by Jack in his pushchair and regularly chatter away to him in shops and in the street. He performs admirably, and I just stand there with my customary inane smile which I hope communicates, 'No, I haven't a clue what you're saying.' I have probably been deluding myself all this time that these avid Spanish baby-talkers are complimenting Jack on how beautiful he is, when really they are making comments such as 'Cor, you're a bald little rascal, aren't

grasp what it was going to be like to be totally responsible for another human being. As it turned out, it was easier to forecast budgets and resources for forthcoming projects at work than to forecast how I would cope with and react to being a mother. If I had had to put a bet on it, I would have lost and the bookies would have been laughing all the way to the bank. However, in my defence, my short-term forecast was more accurate than my long-term forecast – that is, I hit the nail on the head as to how I would feel in those first days that Bethan was at home, but three months down the line it has all changed. I'll explain further.

It was nine o'clock on a Sunday morning, six hours after Bethan had been born, and I was perched on my hospital bed, gazing in disbelief at the little bundle in the cot next to me. This was my new daughter! Then the 'iron maiden' paediatrician stomped down the ward and sternly commanded that I strip the baby ready for inspection, and of course change the nappy, if I hadn't already done so. I trembled at the thought of having to pick up the sleeping babe and, whilst I knew her top from her tail, I couldn't even think of the first thing I needed to do to change her nappy. I felt the tears welling up as I fumbled in my bag to search for cotton wool, nappy and water – '*Water*, where do I get that from and what do I put it in?' I felt panic taking over as I saw the Ayatollah finish examining the baby in the next bed to me. I was next and I still hadn't done the two seemingly simple tasks that she had asked of me. This was my first experience of feeling like an incompetent mother. I felt so helpless. I gathered myself together and gingerly removed the swaddled blanket, the miniature Babygro and the tiny vest. In no time at all, the stern face was looking over me and I shuddered under the belittling gaze. I was being questioned as to why I hadn't changed the nappy, which contained the thick, dark-green meconium, and I heard myself stutter that I didn't know where to get water from, let alone how to change the damn thing. 'Never mind, I'll call a nurse to help you.' Was that a vaguely understanding reply, I wondered? Then she continued with her examination of the now-crying babe. You could have knocked me over with a feather when she proclaimed, 'OK, she is fit and well and you can go home this afternoon.' You would have thought that she had gained three heads, each with bulging eyes and drooling jaws, judging by the response I gave her, with fear etched across my face. 'What, *today*? No, I can't *possibly* go.' I desperately searched for an excuse to stay: 'I haven't even been shown how to bath the baby, never mind feed her!' 'Well, it's up to you.' With that she marched to the next unsuspecting new mum. Fortunately, the midwife came to my rescue and declared that before I could be discharged she wanted to be sure that the baby could feed properly and that I could look after the other tasks, such as topping and tailing, bathing and, finally, nappy changing.

The next twenty-four hours became the first incline of a steep learning curve and my confidence was low. After a second night in hospital without sleep, owing to other babies crying and my own wanting her first proper feed, I decided that I needed my own bed, so I bravely announced the following morning that I wanted to go home. The midwives agreed and arranged for my discharge at three o'clock. Tim came to collect me and we left the maternity unit with Bethan in her car seat and the statutory midwife in tow. I hadn't realized that it is essential for new mums to be escorted off the premises like drunks from the pub, but given the fear I felt at that time, I can appreciate that there must be a risk of finding handfuls of babies outside in the corridor if they didn't actually see them into the car.

The next fiasco was to secure the car seat into the car with the escorting midwife watching. Tim was a bag of nerves and I was no better. As we both fumbled with the straps, I cursed the fact that we hadn't had a practice run prior to this moment. Eventually, after a lot of fumbling, Tim succeeded, and off we set on what seemed to be the longest ride home ever. I was physically shaking as we drew into the drive, and once in the house we set the car seat on the lounge floor, sat back and just stared. Bethan was fast asleep and I felt myself dreading the moment when those eyes would open. I felt utterly helpless, bewildered and frightened – all those things I had thought I would be. I prayed for instinct to take over. It took a while for this to happen, and in those early weeks I found that as soon as I set foot outside the house, whether Bethan was in her pram or her car seat, I had just two basic goals. The first was to get her to fall asleep in one of these two modes of transport, both of which she strongly objected to, and the second was, once asleep, to keep her asleep until I returned to the house (my safe haven) again.

We went for our first major expedition when she was five days old. We were meeting the other girlies and their new babies for lunch in the local wine bar, which was a weekly ritual. Lately it seemed that with each week a new baby had arrived and joined us for lunch, and on this particular day Bethan was the new arrival, which left only Hilary, heavily pregnant and totally fed up. Thankfully, Bethan had dozed off in her car seat, but every time I heard a baby's murmur my heart went into my mouth as I fearfully checked to see if it was Bethan who had woken up. I wasn't ready to cope with her in a public place, and I certainly didn't feel ready to get my boob out and start breastfeeding in such a location. Hilary found my fear quite amusing but also reassuring, as she reckoned she would have the same fears rather than the confidence displayed by Sarah and Annette with Jack and Emily.

Two weeks later, Molly had arrived and we went over to Hilary's house for lunch rather than to the wine bar. Bethan had screamed as per usual as I had put her in the car seat, and I felt myself getting tenser and tenser at the prospect of another outing. She continued to cry in the car, but as we pulled into Hilary's drive her eyes closed and she drifted off to sleep. My task was then to ensure that she did not wake up for the next two hours. In order to achieve this, she was to be left in the seat at all costs, because if I were to lift her out she would wake immediately, unlike the other babies who, when they slept, slept irrespective of their position. So when the first photo-shoot of all the babies was called for, the others were carefully lifted, still sleeping, on to the sofa and laid down in ascending order of age. Bethan was to lie between Jack and Molly, but rather than disturb her from her sleep, I kept her in her car seat. So there it is for posterity, the photo that shows Queen Bethan (as she became known) in her throne, with her subjects lying next to her. All because I was too scared to move her!

Now, three months down the line, I am far more confident with Bethan, and that first nappy change and the tears seem so far away. I knew that the first few weeks would be a learning curve but I was never sure whether I would ever reach the top of it. I never guessed that I would feel as comfortable as I now do in the role of mother. As I said at the beginning of this section, my perspective has completely changed, which is something I had never imagined possible.

I have actually become so adept at this motherhood business, and all the baby conversations that go with it, that it has become quite frightening on some occasions. One of these conversations specifically springs to mind. It was our first girls' night out together, without babies, as we were giving Annette a send-off before she returned to work. We chatted eagerly and exchanged experiences, advice and stories about our children. I then found myself saying, 'I wish Shane Ritchie would come around to my front door to examine my whites! I'd give him a challenge for his camera and he could prove to me that his washing powder could shift my stubborn stains! Thank God I'm using disposable nappies, otherwise I hate to think of the state of Bethan's under-carriage with my current washing powder, and as for cleaning Tim's shirt collars, it –' I stopped myself mid-flow at this point, as I saw the look of total disbelief on the faces around me. I had spent the last ten minutes talking about washing powders, and by the looks I was getting it had been nine minutes too long. Andrea had humoured me by warning me about the perils of pureed-carrot stains, which I didn't even want to think about, but even she had come to her senses five minutes previously and was equally as dazed as the rest of the group. 'Sorry, I got carried away,' I sheepishly apologized, then took a slurp of wine and waited for the conversation to start again. I did find myself wondering, though, how on earth our mothers and grandmothers coped before the invention of biological powders. Perhaps they never gave us carrots, and used paper bags inside those terry nappies. I must ask my mum. I would like to justify this horrendously uncharacteristic outburst of motherly/housewifely conversation by claiming that it relates to my research on wool, but I would be lying. I think I have just become frighteningly maternal!

I have also found that I have become more emotional, and I am now sensitive to any issues concerning children which, prior to Bethan's birth, might have passed me by. I find myself welling up with tears at the slightest thing on TV, and any begging mail that arrives on my doormat with a picture of an innocent child in need on it always gets the donation it requests. To this end, I congratulate the marketing people at charities such as the NSPCC, who obviously have access to the names and addresses of new, full-of-emotion mums, and send their envelopes, with the £10-donation request, to reach these people at the same time as the free nappy or baby-product vouchers. They have now succeeded where once they would have failed, and I certainly would never have predicted that I would become emotional enough to fall prey to such tactics.

Annette

***

Having read all the books and got on first-name terms with all of the midwives at the maternity unit, and even acted as a twenty-four-hour parental advisor for Andrea over *her* new arrival's nappy content, I was just desperate to take ownership of *my* baby. Finally, my day came.

The realization that we now 'owned' a baby really hit us both hard on our first night at home. Emily suddenly wanted feeding constantly, developed colic and screamed like a banshee non-stop. She sucked on my breasts until they seemed raw. To this day I still have no idea whether any milk was coming out or not, but at least it stopped the screaming for a while. That first night I felt panic-stricken – we now had a noisy little person living with us, who looked as though she would be keeping us up every night for evermore. How on earth were we going to survive? How was our marriage going to survive? Would we ever have a sex life again? We were already frayed around the edges and a dirty great tear seemed imminent. This was just the beginning and I could already see myself as a twitching, gibbering, divorced single mother with only a screaming child for company! By midday on day two, I had pulled myself together and decided that it was down to me to prevent this screaming new midget from wrecking my marriage. I have always been opposed to live-in nannies and au pairs, but if that was what it was going to take, I would have to consider it. I would even have considered a live-in Relate Counsellor at this stage.

However, somehow over the following nights and weeks, I seemed to develop the patience of a saint and just rose above the sleep deprivation and stress. Gavin still cannot understand it. Usually without sleep I am nothing short of Hannibal Lecter, but motherhood somehow transformed me from Lecter to Lamb. I had someone else to worry about now, who was relying on me 100 per cent, and losing my cool was just not going to get me anywhere. Gavin was good at recognizing the signs when I did finally get a little frayed around the edges and would take Emily off my hands for a while.

As Emily started settling into solid blocks of sleep at night, Gavin was horrified to discover that his sleep pattern remained equally disrupted by my half-hourly paranoid baby patrol. Stage one – I would wake up in a cold sweat, adamant that Emily must still be somewhere in the bed, and with one fell swoop I would toss my sleeping husband out of bed like a caber and then crawl around the mattress, dementedly patting every inch. Once the mattress had been exhausted there was, of course, the entire surrounding floor area to check. By the time I had allowed Gavin back into the cold bed, content that my search was fruitless and that Emily must be safely settled in her cot after all, I would be wide awake.

Commence stage two of paranoid baby patrol. Emily has been asleep for a long time. I wonder if I should check her? But she might be disturbed if I check her. I'll leave it. But what if she is cold? Or she might be overheating. Did I tuck those sheets in tight enough? She could have been sick. She might have choked. She could have had a fit, for all I know. Anything could have happened.

At this point, I would give in to my paranoia and go and check her, realizing that I had no hope of my brain switching to sleep mode until all of these questions had been answered. As I was finally able to snuggle contentedly down to a decent snooze, I would feel that distinctive surge as my breasts filled up and feed-time loomed fast. Here we go again.

When it comes to baby talk, Gavin beats me hands down. All the way through pregnancy he was full of bizarre advice, and on several occasions he impressed both Andrea and me with useful tips. For example, drinking raspberry-leaf tea and consuming linseed oil apparently helps you during labour. The baby should glide out and you rarely need stitches. Interestingly, both Sarah and I consumed gallons of raspberry-leaf tea, and did not require a single stitch between us!

The most useful tip he came up with related to when you have a full bladder but are unable to empty it fully due to the positioning of the baby. One afternoon I was sitting on the toilet grumbling about this, and Gavin merrily blurted out that if I were to rock gently backwards and forwards and from side to side, this would relieve the pressure slightly and enable me to empty my bladder. I looked at him in amazement. 'How on earth do you know that?' 'Oh, we were discussing it at work!' By *we* I thought perhaps someone at work was pregnant and had been going into specific details with him, but no. '*We*' actually meant him and five other men, who had sat around gossiping over their morning cups of coffee, sharing their parental experiences in the minutest detail. Gavin had obviously been moaning to them about me continuously getting up during the night to go to the toilet. They in turn had shared the delights of forceps deliveries, stirrups and stitches. When I discovered just how useful this tip was that he had picked up, I decided to hold back from exploding at him for sharing my private details with his work colleagues – but I made a mental note to avoid office parties in the future!

Before I fell pregnant, I was not really interested in babies at all, and the thought of sitting around talking about nappies seemed unimaginable. But now my views have changed slightly. At work and home, with friends and family, a large proportion of my time is spent talking about Emily. It is difficult to avoid the subject, though, because everyone asks about her. I am always conscious not to talk about her too much, but when I try and change the subject people change it back again. I can't win!

The one thing I really took a strong dislike to was the antenatal reunions. Everyone sits around with their new pride and joy, but with absolutely nothing else in common. Then the comparisons in baby development start. 'Does your baby do this yet? Does your baby do that yet?' It is all so superficial and competitive, but I still found myself coming away thinking, 'My God, my baby weighs too much,' or 'She is not developing properly.' I soon came down to earth again, though, and trained myself to think, 'Who cares? She looks healthy and is happy and content. She will do her own thing in her own good time.' I am sure that if, for some reason, you were to compare the same children when they reached eighteen, you would not be able to pick out the child who had cut a tooth first from the crowd!

Below the Belt

Bowels, bladders and bleeding – both ours and our babies' – became a key feature in our conversations from very shortly after the births.

We were all amazed, or should I say horrified, at just how soon we slipped into the sad situation of studying with such fascination the toilet habits of another human being. Having proudly boasted that our friendship existed despite our babies, and that our conversations did not and would not revolve totally around our new little charges, we found ourselves spending what amounted to the best part of a whole afternoon, shortly after our babies' births, talking about nothing but the contents of their nappies. There we were, five professional women, all respected and valued in our own industries, plummeting to such depths in such a short space of time. Very frightening.

These conversations inevitably led on to discussions about our own bodily functions, something we certainly had never imagined discussing with friends over coffee. But as our bodies had been through such upheaval, it is hardly surprising that we sought reassurance from our new-found soulmates that all of these south-of-navel nightmares were normal.

Hilary

* * *

I seem to have a whole host of gory anecdotes about the various events which occurred in my knickers during and after my pregnancy. I am not sure if I am just preoccupied with pants, periods and poos, or if I had particularly nasty experiences, but here goes.

Firstly, although not strictly below the belt, I had a bit of a vomiting problem during my labour. Before giving birth, I had been totally obsessed with the fear of pooing during labour, but nobody had warned me of the puking possibility too. Well, as the labour progressed and the big pushing moment drew closer, suddenly the fear of fouling the delivery couch went out of the window and I really would not have given a damn if I had produced a full-blown cowpat. I still don't know if I actually did have a bowel movement, but if I did everyone was extremely discreet and gas masks were not applied, so it can't have been that bad. However, as David and I savoured the magical moment when the midwife left the room, leaving us to soak up every detail of our perfect new daughter, I suddenly had an extremely urgent need to vomit. David managed to grab a puke bowl and rescue Molly from the firing line just in the nick of time. I don't want to turn stomachs with graphic details, but what I produced was almost black in colour and I quickly sent David on a hunt for a midwife, fearing that this was blood and I had suffered internal bleeding. I have never felt such a prune as when the midwife returned and casually pointed out that masticated banana in hot tea tended to look like this. She said that, much as she was always grateful for gifts following the delivery of a baby, she generally preferred chocolates or flowers to bowls of puke and a quick round of 'Guess What I Ate?'.

The list we'd been given telling us what to pack in our hospital bags said to take old or disposable knickers, and a packet of high-absorbency sanitary towels. I had anticipated the equivalent of a heavy period postnatally, and naïvely thought that I would get through about three of these sanitary towels a day, not three an hour and all at once! Nothing short of a king-size fifteen-tog duvet stuffed between my legs would realistically have done the job adequately. It was as though God had put his wicked sense of humour into action and said, 'Right, well if I am going to give them nine months off menstruation, how about I give them all those missed periods at once at the end?' Anyone who believes that God is a woman has obviously not been through the experience of pregnancy and childbirth! Well, all this made a complete mockery of the notion that you could support the required quantity of padding between your legs with a pair of your old knickers. Unless your old knickers happen to be the size of the average marquee, forget it!

I had the additional pleasure of having what the midwife excitedly termed a 'dirty Duncan' placenta. This apparently means that the enormous lump of liver, which I gave birth to after my daughter, came out inside-out. Don't ask me how or why, but apparently this creates a higher chance of blood clots, because the placenta may not have had a clean break from the uterus. Sure enough, four days later, I suddenly found myself adopting the bent-over hip-wriggling contraction pose as an enormous stomach cramp took hold, and five minutes later I found that I had given birth to a huge lump of raspberry jelly. It was nearly the size of my hand – I know this because I had to catch it and save it in a pot for the midwife to look at the following day! I must be the least popular new mum in the area. I seem to be constantly saving disgusting bodily functions for inspection. I would not be surprised if there was a note in my file to all prospective visiting midwives saying, 'Don't, whatever you do, accept a chocolate from this woman, as it may well turn out to be a sample of her *faeces*!'

I had not appreciated before going through the experience of childbirth just how easily I could lose my inhibitions, although I must admit I gained an inkling of this when Sarah so casually detailed her bowel movements to me when I asked her how she was feeling three days after giving birth to Jack. That is a different story altogether, though, and one I will leave for her to tell.

Along with the prospect of pooing in labour, my second major fear was losing my bladder control postnatally. This was a very real fear, as I have never had particularly strong bladder muscles, and among close friends and family, who have the ability to make me laugh hysterically, I am known to have the occasional accident. These usually occur at moments of hilarity, generally after a few beers and when I have been too interested in what is going on to go to the toilet for many hours on end. The most memorable occasion (when, I hasten to add, I happened to be sober) was a few years ago, when my mother and I went to London to try on wedding dresses. My mother has the ability to send me into hysterics with one simple change in facial expression, especially when in the company of people with a distinct lack of sense of humour. So, as we stood in an extremely upmarket bridal parlour with me dressed in a horrendous blanc-mange number which made me look like a bloke in drag, my mother passed some inane comment while the cooing assistant went off to find a tiara or something to finish off my toilet-roll-fairy appearance. It was just enough to trigger a bout of silent hysteria, which I desperately tried to gain control over before the twinset-and-pearls middle-aged assistant reappeared. Sud-denly, the huge fizzy drink I had consumed at lunchtime decided it was time to make its exit. In a desperate bid to win the battle I was having with my bladder muscles, I stuffed my hands between my legs. Regaining composure, I released the oodles of material that I had shoved between my legs, only to discover that the battle had been lost – there, in a huge dark circle on the front of the blancmange bridal gown, was the tell-tale sign that my bladder had achieved its evacuation aim. I don't think that either my mum or I have ever moved so quickly. I was out of the frock, dressed and gone before the poor assistant could say 'diamante or pearls', leaving the froufrou frock hanging between half a dozen others in the vain hope that it would dry out before being discovered.

Well, as you can imagine, with a bladder this weak before childbirth, my fear was quite justified. I became the Pelvic-Floor Princess. I did quick bursts of pelvic-floor exercises all day every day, amounting to a minimum of two hundred a day, and I am proud to say that I could have star jumped (the ultimate test) with confidence from the day after I gave birth, if my boobs would have let me! I haven't as yet been in the full-bladder, few-beers, full-blown-hysteria predicament, which to me will be the ultimate test of just how effective all those pelvic-floor exercises were, and so I wait with bated breath to see if at twenty-nine I am now fully toilet trained!

Well, that is enough on *my* nappy contents. Now to Molly's. Before having a baby, I certainly had not appreciated just how much pleasure I could get from another person having a bowel movement. Poor Molly really has struggled with her digestive system. When I was totally breastfeeding, if I so much as looked at a curry, even a mild korma, she got tummy pains. She is either going constantly or can't go for days. When I see her little face take on that 'this is it' expression and all her concentration goes into that bearing-down motion, I can't help feeling sorry for her. She goes bright red, and grunts and groans almost as much as I did in second-stage labour. I have even taken to cheering her on: 'Come on, baby, you can do it – just one more push!' I think I know how David felt now – you're just so helpless!

Well, when her efforts actually pay off, then comes the proud inspection of the nappy, passing judgement on quantity, aroma and consistency. After the initial blacky-coloured poos, they went to plain yellow, both of which I was fully prepared for, but when at the end of the first week they suddenly had bits in I panicked! It looked just like wholegrain mustard, and coinciden- tally I had eaten mustard the night before. David jokingly said, 'I told you not to eat that last night. Look what you've done to her now!' This sent me straight into guilt-trip panic mode, and once again a package was saved for the midwife's inspection. I don't think there has ever been a midwife as grateful to sign a woman off her books after ten days as mine was!

David is still concerned that I have an unhealthy obsession with Molly's bowels, but I console myself that this must be a 'new mum' thing. On many occasions, when meeting up with the girlies, I have overheard the tail end of a conversation between Andrea and Lyndsey comparing notes on Max and Bethan's motions, so I know I am not alone.

Andrea

* * *

Call me naïve, but although I had anticipated childbirth to be messy, I had not anticipated blood loss to be quite such a memorable experience. I was about ten minutes away from giving birth when the midwife decided that I should try to empty my bladder, because it was holding things up. She instructed Bruce to accompany me to the toilet, so off we went. I could not have peed for love or money at this stage in the proceedings, but it was a really comfortable position so I stayed there through a few contractions until Bruce, in a panic that Max was about to be born and christened in one fell swoop, forced me back to the delivery suite. What we had not realized was that I was now bleeding, and Bruce, following me, managed to spread a delightfully rich red trail of footprints all over the delivery suite! Once he had noticed what was happening, he then started tiptoeing around like Wayne Sleep in trainers, in a desperate and fruitless mission to reduce the spread until he had cleaned his soles. By the time the midwife returned, the delivery suite looked more like a scene from a Hammer House of Horror film than a tranquil setting for childbirth!

Ten minutes after giving birth, I found myself having a domestic-dementia experience just like Hilary, and was on my hands and knees cleaning everything up – shower, toilet and delivery room. I had heard that pregnant women go in for 'nesting' before their babies are born. All I can say is that I think my nesting instincts were somewhat delayed. I wonder if the NHS relies on this to save its housekeeping budget!

I had, like all expectant mothers, followed the checklist of things to pack for hospital to the letter, weeks in advance of my due date, but when it said to pack sanitary towels I did not realize quite how many I had to get. I ended up relying on the ones the hospital provided until Bruce was able and brave enough to go out and purchase me some super-duper mega-absorbency ones. I have to say that the NHS ones were about as much use as a chocolate teapot, basically they were a little bit of cotton wool held together with what looked like a cheap string-vest, so Bruce was instructed to get brave very early on! I had also dutifully purchased the disposable maternity knickers and was very pleased that I had taken Flash Your Knickers Fiona's advice and got them a couple of sizes too big. Even then, every time I hoisted them up I managed to stick my finger through them, and I am hardly one for glamorous pointed nails! The knickers were, after all, nothing more than a couple of bits of paper glued together. Had I realized this before I bought them, I reckon I could have saved some money by putting my Blue Peter skills into practice and making some for myself out of an old newspaper and some sticky-backed plastic! They weren't really suitable for the job they were intended for, but they did match the string-vest sanitary towel nicely. I soon gave up on them, though, and spent the next couple of weeks wearing my football knickers, which were a bit hardier, having been used for sliding around in all weather conditions.

The next below-the-belt nightmare I met concerned having my first postnatal poo! Having had stitches, I was certain that they had put too many in and not left room for the emptying of the bowels. I kept wanting to go, but I was petrified in case all of the stitches and everything that they were holding together would come exploding out with the pressure. I would sit on the toilet for ages, but nothing happened. Eventually, after about three days, I proudly popped out the equivalent of a rabbit dropping, and this was how things went on for about a week until I felt brave enough to go properly. It was a very pleasant relief when I knew that everything was still in one piece after this toilet event. I had not appreciated how triumphant an event giving birth to a poo could be!

Talking of pooing, this changed slightly during the first few months after Max's birth. I had always had a reasonably good advance-warning system of when one was due, and I knew that I had a good hour or two before I would need to be rushing to find a toilet. This changed somewhat after giving birth, and when I needed to go it really did mean *now*! I literally had to find a toilet immediately. Bruce is very pleased that this only lasted a couple of months, because he was getting fed up with me interrupting his morning bathroom routine by kicking him out so that I could go!

There definitely does appear to be a postnatal period of dignity loss — well, there was for me. Suddenly all of my personal issues seemed to become public property. I am not entirely sure whether it was loss of my dignity or loss of my marbles I experienced when the midwife came to see me the day after I came out of hospital. I was sitting in my lounge with a couple of friends (luckily close friends!) and Bruce. After the midwife had checked over Max, she suddenly pinged on the infamous rubber gloves and gleefully announced that it was 'time to check mummy'. By the time I had scanned the room to see whether my mother had arrived unannounced, not yet having grasped the concept of me being a mum, the midwife was looking ready for action. The gloves were a dead give-away as to what bits of mummy she wanted to check, and before I knew it I was lying on my sofa with my legs akimbo for all my guests to see. Talk about daytime viewing! I tell you, Richard and Judy had nothing on this visual spectacular! Both friends suddenly developed a deep fascination with my wallpaper and Bruce took a nosedive into the sports pages of the newspaper. Retrospectively, the most baffling thing of all, I now realize, is that I said absolutely nothing. Me, a police officer, trained to handle the most difficult of situations in a confident and controlled manner, could not even manage to muster up the presence of mind to say, 'Do you mind if we go somewhere a bit more private?' Talk about spongy brain! I think childbirth must have had a frightening effect on my inhibitions!

Fortunately, this mental disruption was a temporary ailment, otherwise I dread to think of the devastatingly disruptive repercussions it could have had at the Arsenal games this season. I reckon I would have been doing a full-blown Erica Roe–style streak at every available opportunity.

Annette

* * *

Wees seemed to be a major feature of my pregnancy. Firstly, carrying that increasingly ammonia-stenched little pot to and from all appointments, for the midwives to dip their little sticks into. Most memorable, though, was going for a scan. 'Please arrive with a full bladder,' the scan card says, but I had no idea quite what an art it is to get your bladder full enough for the scanning person's satisfaction, but not so full that you can't move without threatening to flood the waiting-room. You can guarantee that the day you arrive for your appointment already bursting for a wee, the hospital will be running at least one hour behind schedule, and you will be left sitting in the waiting-room, a shivering, sweating, uncomfortable cross-legged mess with hallucinations of toilets flashing before your eyes. Yet if you turn up early clutching your jumbo-sized bottle of mineral water, ready to do battle with it to fill your bladder just in time for your appointment, then they will be running ahead of schedule and before you know it you will have been on and off the scan table, chastized and sent like a naughty schoolgirl back to the waiting-room to 'do as you're told and fill your bladder'.

I also have painful memories of the first time I passed water after I had given birth. The first hurdle was standing up and trying to walk after being laid on my back for hours. I was feeling extremely delicate all over, which wasn't helped by the undignified way I was hauled off the bed on to my feet in a similar fashion to James Herriot sorting out a cow that's 'gone down'. Fortunately ropes were not required, though! I felt weak and faint, and I cannot describe the feeling between my legs, but it was as though nothing short of a massacre had taken place down there. Somehow in this weak and pathetic state I managed to hobble my way to the bathroom with the assistance of the midwife.

Amazingly, despite the physical and emotional wreck I had become, my life-long public-toilet phobia remained fully intact, and much to the midwife's astonishment I still chose the hovering rather than sitting option! It seemed a lifetime that I squatted, with knees trembling, over that pan watching oodles of gunk and blood come out, but eventually I came to the conclusion that in amongst that lot I must have passed urine at some point, and headed for the shower.

How wrong I was. Halfway through my shower, the familiar sensation of needing a wee returned and at the midwife's recommendation I started to pass urine in the shower. All I can say is that there is not a word in the English language which quantifies quite how much urine stings when it is passing over open wounds – but boy does it sting! Tears streamed down my face and I felt so timid and pathetic, but the midwife seemed quite unfazed as she helped me to dry off and hobble back to bed, as if this was standard behaviour from all new mums.

Well, that's enough about my bladder. Now to Emily's nappy contents. Emily is a complete gannet when it comes to food, particularly when she was being breastfed. She put on loads of weight and looked a picture of health. However, her nappies were a different story altogether. Their contents were bright green and looked more like something produced by an alien than by my perfect little daughter. If you consult any textbook, it warns that green nappies are a sign of malnutrition. Common sense should have told me that there was no way that Emily was suffering from malnutrition, as she piled on the pounds rather than ounces, but I still went off into first-time-mother panic mode and offered my poor starved child constant food. After inflicting a view of these evil specimens on visiting friends and relatives for them to pass comment on, to no avail, I decided to do the sensible thing and show the health visitor. The reason for the green nappies turned out to be quite the opposite to malnutrition. Emily was guzzling so much milk so quickly that her system was in fact not having enough time to digest the food properly before the next feed came along, so was simply forcing it straight out to make room for the next meal!

Emily could have won awards for the speed at which she could catapult a poo out of her backside, as well. I tell you, Exocet missiles have been known to move slower than Emily's poos. I will never forget changing her nappy late one night. When I took the nappy off, there was a huge gush of wind very shortly followed by a high-flying turd. Normally, I would try and catch it using the nappy as a makeshift baseball mitt, but because I was tired my fielding skills were not up to premier-league standards. When I looked across the room, there was the explosive mess all over the walls and dripping down to the floor in great globules. Luckily we had polished floorboards in Emily's room, as I think it would have been a re-carpeting job otherwise. Unfortunately, the wallpaper did not come off as lightly and required a fresh coat of paint and an artistic stencil effect to disguise the incident!

Sarah

* * *

I innocently thought that I could get through my pregnancy wearing very small knickers, but I quickly found out why there are specific maternity knickers on the market. With my normal knickers, I soon found that the gusset was ending up far further under than was functional, and considering that I found that discharge increased whilst I was pregnant, the correct gusset location was quite important! I ended up buying some quite hideous maternity pants, which far surpassed any of my previous granny knickers. Tim fondly nicknames any of my underwear with so much as a millimetre too much fabric 'parachute knickers', but I think these monstrosities would have held up an entire parachute regiment. It has to be said, though, that what these purpose-made maternity knickers lack in sex appeal (they stretch over your bump, and virtually up to your armpits) they certainly make up for in comfort. They offer Lycra support to the ever-increasing bump, and also give you a bit more warmth on those draughty days when you've ventured out wearing a maternity marquee. All I can say is, thank heavens for Lycra, otherwise maternity pants would have to be sold with braces.

Thank heavens for Lycra, otherwise maternity pants would have to be sold with braces

I did manage to avoid wearing these knickers when I tried a spot of sunbathing in the back garden when I was heavily pregnant. I had read somewhere that the hormones and chemicals

The Fat Ladies Club

floating around a woman's body when she's pregnant made her tan more easily. As I am normally quite a paleface, I was keen to give this theory a shot and make good use of the start of my maternity leave, so that I wouldn't look too pale and pasty for the inevitable hospital photos of mother and new baby. In addition, I was not holding out too much hope of being able to sunbathe once the baby had arrived. I organized my relaxing afternoon with military precision and installed myself in a secluded part of the garden with a good book and my sunglasses, wearing nothing but a skimpy bikini and a sarong. As I lay there, marvelling at how much better my larger chest looked in my underwired bikini top, I was caught off-guard completely by an unexpected visit from my best friend's husband. I now look back with horror at the scene. I did not even have the decency to cover myself up with a T-shirt. My lack of inhibition must have either been due to a mild case of sunstroke, a wild desire to show off my new-found cleavage to all and sundry, or quite simply that innocent oblivion that pregnant women seem to have about the size of their bodies. I'm sure it was the latter, because I don't remember feeling any embarrassment at all as I stood chatting away, wearing little more than what amounted to a bra, pants and an enormous stomach. It all seemed perfectly natural at the time to me, but it must have been a frightening eye-opener to my friend's husband, who, not being a father himself, had probably never experienced the full enormity of a thirty-eight-week-pregnant woman in the bare flesh! It was only afterwards that I realized that the poor chap had looked as though he was wearing a whiplash collar all the time he was talking to me, not daring to move his head up and down for fear that his eyes would have to follow. For the entire conversation his eyes never wavered from eye-level.

Another perfectly natural moment was when Hilary called me a few days after I had left hospital, to ask me how it had all gone. During the conversation she asked me how my motions were. I instantly launched into a blow-by-blow account of my bowel movements over the last couple of days, without any inhibition whatsoever, but as my detailed description came to an end the silence at the other end of the phone made me a little uneasy. 'No, you dozy tart,' Hilary blurted out. 'I wanted to know how your *emotions* are, not your bowel *motions*!' Suddenly I couldn't believe what I had actually been saying to this relatively new friend. If in a sane moment I had described such details to someone as close as my mother it would have been out of character, but to a new acquaintance! Thank heavens she is a nurse. Fortunately, at this point my emotions were still reasonably strong. If we'd had the same conversation a week later I'm sure I'd have responded with a torrent of tears rather than howls of laughter.

One thing that has pleased Tim immensely about having a baby around is that someone else in the house is now farting and burping as loudly as (and arguably more frequently than) he is. Never having had a dog to take the blame for such bodily functions (and neither of our cats fart audibly), it is great all of a sudden to be able to blame them on a baby instead. What is laughable is the fact that we congratulate Jack on his every expulsion of gas, something which I am sure will only last until he understands what he is doing! Can you imagine Jack at his first church nativity, dressed as a shepherd, proudly burping along to 'Good King Wenceslas', periodically applauding himself and crying 'result' and 'clever Munchkin' to the audience – how mortifying for his parents! Jack's farting has, however, let me down badly a couple of times in public. One occasion was when I was in a DIY shop buying some glass. I had slipped into the shop with Jack in his car seat and placed him safely at my feet beside the counter. The guy arrived from out the back and, while I explained to him the dimensions of the glass I needed, Jack let out a stream of blistering, earth-tremoring farts. They were made more audible by the way they reverberated into his car seat. I carried on regardless, and then realized to my dismay that the bloke was looking at me in disbelief. He couldn't see Jack at my a desperate bid to avoid the chronic indigestion induced by toe-touching. OK, I realize that this is not strictly below the belt, but after Bethan was born these organs certainly felt as though they were on their way to a bottomless pit. It is quite difficult to explain how I felt when Bethan evacuated the space she had stolen from them, but if you can imagine taking a ride in a lift in a sky-scraper which plummets from the penthouse floor to the basement within seconds, you will begin to get the idea! It is hardly surprising really, though – after all, these organs had been increasingly compressed and squeezed upwards as the baby had gradually grown and then, within the space of minutes, they had been released. It was as though they were bursting out of their confined space shouting 'Surprise!' and then partying in my gut, which was now equivalent in size to the Albert Hall!

I did have one delicate below-the-belt complaint which I was unlucky enough to suffer from during pregnancy, and that was a mild case of haemorrhoids – piles. They appeared around about my twenty-fourth week of pregnancy but, contrary to what I was expecting, disappeared around week thirty-seven. In fact, when I had eventually plucked up the courage to mention them to the doctor at around week thirty-two, she gave me the usual advice to try and prevent constipation. That is, to drink plenty of fluids, eat lots of fibre and so on. But rather than offering reassurance that they would go away, she said, 'They are probably going to get worse before they get better, what with the strain of childbirth, and you may find them even more aggravated in the days after the birth.' That was it, I thought. I'll have to make a concerted effort to get rid of these. Whatever I did seemed to do the trick and fortunately they disappeared a couple of weeks before Bethan was born. As I pushed and strained during labour, the thought of the recurrence of piles entered my head for a fleeting moment. It then became a major concern as I awaited my first bowel movement following the birth. To my utter amazement, when this did arrive it was pain- and pile-free, and what a relief that was, in more ways than one, if you get my drift!

Where Do We Go from Here?

Well, all of our babies are now somewhere between four months and five and a half months old, and we have all survived to tell this tale. It is almost impossible to remember what life really felt like before our new additions. We began this book by telling you where we all started from, what we did, and how we felt about our pending parenthood. It seems only fitting, therefore, to conclude by telling you how we feel *now*, and where we see our lives going from here.

How are we finding motherhood? How has it hit our relationships? What about returning to work? What about future children?

I think that we have all been knocked sideways by the changes in ourselves and our attitudes towards babies since giving birth to our own. We just hope that, if you have felt any of the same fears and trepidations that we voiced at the beginning, you will be consoled by the realization that there is life after babies. We also hope that you will come out of this amazing experience of motherhood feeling even half as positive as we all do.

Hilary

* * *

I never thought that I would be able to say this, but I am thoroughly enjoying being a mother and have not found the experience at all stressful so far!

Molly is now four months old, and every morning I am thrilled to see her. Even with the occasional morning starting at four I feel nothing but pleasure, and tiredness of course, when she greets

me with her huge morning grin. Parental love is unbelievable –
I could never have imagined it would be so intense and strong.
This doesn't mean that we are putting Molly up on some kind
of pedestal of perfection, but we simply love her for who she is.
She will never be the dainty little doll that Bethan is, or a cuddly
bundle that sleeps twelve hours a night like Emily. She will never
dish out smiles that would light up lives as willingly as Max and
Jack always do, but she will always be our Molly with all her
own funny little quirks. David and I are closer than we have ever
been, and all in all everything is viewed through rose-tinted
glasses in our house at the moment. I'm just waiting for this
fantastic bubble to burst!

I have been in the fortunate position of not having to rush
back to work, which has been a huge bonus. I am due to return
to my post when Molly is just over seven months old, but on a
part-time basis only. This, I think, will be just about the perfect
time, as long as I manage to persuade Molly that she doesn't want
to breastfeed any more by then. So much for my twelve-weeks-
breastfeeding-only policy! I am just beginning now to crave the
adult company and responsibilities of my job again and, to be
quite honest, I am missing my clients! I have not actually worked
out childcare arrangements, but my plan is to find a childminder
for two days a week, and David or my mum will look after Molly
on the third day. I think the lure of the four-day weekend is part
of the pull to return to work. After all, my working week will
be so short it will hardly be a major strain!

I am quite worried though about the effect having a baby will
have had on my emotional ability to cope with my clients'
disabilities. Before Molly, I always found it really easy to focus
on my clients' abilities rather than their disabilities, which is so
essential in doing my job well. Yet, since having Molly, I have
turned into complete emotional mush at the sight of any disabilities. I find myself bursting into tears of sympathy at things
like Children in Need. I just hope my positive practice re-
emerges when I get back into the swing of things, otherwise my

poor clients are not going to know what has hit them when I start blubbering every time I visit.

The next major hassle in our lives, before the return-to-work hurdle, will be the skiing holiday we have coming up. The prospect of flights, coaches, cold weather, leaving Molly with a nanny service and getting her to sleep in a strange cot are all worries I daren't think about or I would immediately cancel the holiday and settle for a week of videos, take-aways and slobbing out at home, which sounds altogether far more relaxing to me!

I have not actually managed to go out for an evening in the past month because of Molly's eating habits. She has taken to finishing her final feed of the evening at about ten o'clock and will *only* have the breast at that time. We have tried everything in our power to break this habit, but unfortunately she has beaten all of our babysitters to date, and after one and a half hours of solid screaming they have all given in and called us home again. However, the battle continues and I do intend to win this one; hopefully before her sixteenth birthday! The only problem is that I think I have forgotten how to socialize, and poor David has had to handle my verbal diarrhoea alone! I think that is why the poor chap has taken to going to bed before me. He's exhausted just listening to me each night!

As for brothers and sisters for Molly, yes, I hope so. David always joked that he wanted a minimum of five babies and at least three girls, and I always said that I might stretch to two children, if he was lucky! Well, much as I hate to let a man win, if all goes well for us, I think the final figure will be nearer to his estimation than mine. I desperately want a large family now, and have agreed to start trying for number two on Molly's first birthday.

It really grates me to say this, but I think I must finally concede that I am now bordering on being the earth-mother-type person that I so boldly mocked before Molly's birth. I won't be stretching to the kaftan frocks, home-birthing pool and belly dancing at the birth of my next baby, but breastfeeding, baby talk and the battle of the bulge are all activities I can't wait to embark on again, and again, and again!

Lyndsey

* * *

At the end of the day, I am not too sure where we will go from here. Before Bethan arrived I had it all planned. Following twenty-nine weeks' maternity leave, I would return to work and Bethan would go to a nursery. In fact, the company I work for offers a 'phase-in' scheme for the first six months, which means I would not be going back full-time until Bethan is one year old. It seemed so black and white at the time, but what I did not take into account was that, first of all, I would have such an adorable little girl, and, second, that my emotions would now be a player in the decision-making process. If Bethan was a little monster who screamed all day I might be begging to go back to work early, but she is such a happy baby it is a pleasure to be with her. I never thought that my emotions would get the better of me and that I would actually want to stay at home twenty-four hours a day with a baby. She has ruined all my plans and I now dread the day that I have to return to work.

I had also decided before Bethan was born that she would go to a nursery, and thought no more about it. That was that, decision made. What I hadn't bargained for was how I would feel when I was viewing prospective nurseries when Bethan was about six weeks old. One place in particular had a secluded baby room, and as I was leaving I took another peep through the small glass window in the door and saw a tiny baby sitting crying on his own in a baby ring – talk about tugging at the heart strings! It took all my effort to keep my composure, say my goodbyes and take the first available exit. As I drove home I had tears in my eyes imagining that that little baby was Bethan, and I realized that this was not going to be as black and white as I had imagined six months previously. I must add that the next nursery I visited was completely different and I came out feeling slightly more positive about the idea.

It has been consoling to see how well both Annette and Emily have coped with Annette's premature return to work. This has inevitably made the imminent step of childcare slightly easier for me to bear, but I am glad that I still have three months to go before my four-day working week starts.

I do not like to look too far into the future, as I am conscious of how quickly the years are disappearing. Before Bethan was born she was to be our one and only child. Tim and I were quite convinced about that. However, even in her few weeks on this earth, I find she is growing so quickly, and each developmental milestone seems to be arriving and passing with such haste that I can already feel myself thinking that it would be lovely to have another baby to enjoy this time again with. But four months is not long enough to blot out the memory of childbirth, and it will take a bit more than sentimentality before I consider going through that experience again.

Andrea

* * *

I will always remember my mother saying to me during my pregnancy paranoia stage, 'If you are worried now before the birth, just wait until your baby arrives – you will worry for the next twenty years or so.' I shrugged off the thought, deciding that my mum had always been a bit mad, due to her Mediterranean blood. I recalled the days in my teenage years when she would not sleep at night until all of her three children were safely home from their nights out. She would then nag at us and say, 'Just you wait until you have children of your own!' I have to confess that now, after just five and a half months, I know exactly how she must have felt. It is difficult to describe exactly how strong the feelings for a newborn child are, but it is a totally different kind of love from that for a partner. I can best describe it as a protective sort of emotion. My feelings towards Max of wanting to protect and look after him at any cost are totally new to me and, as a policewoman, it concerns me to think that I would be capable of killing someone who harmed my son.

The smiles that a baby gives are so unconditional and genuine, and when Max greets us with a big grin it always brightens up our day. When a baby smiles it is guaranteed to be indicative of nothing but a totally genuine pleasure to see you.

When I first fell pregnant, Bruce and I decided that we would save like mad for the whole nine months so that I would be able to take some unpaid leave after the statutory three months had expired. I am so pleased that we did this as it has meant that I will be going back to work when Max is around seven months old. I have enjoyed my first few months at home with Max, but right from the beginning I always felt that I would want to go back to work. Not just for financial reasons, but also for the challenge and stimulation work provides. My career ambitions, however, have totally changed! Before Max arrived, I had spent almost two years on a squad that dealt with drug offences, and it was a very busy and rewarding period of my career. The next natural progressive step for me would have been a placement in CID, and that was very much the direction in which I wanted to head. This has all changed now, and my career ambitions will have to take second place to my family. The thought of having to stop a tape-recorded interview with a suspect in order to arrange for someone to collect Max from the nursery for me would, I fear, not go down too well with my supervisors! With this in mind, I will be going back to work now in the slightly less dramatic role of a community bobby in a local town. Whether I am right to hope that this will not feel like a complete come-down and that I will be able to adjust and enjoy it, only time will tell. The work will still be varied and challenging, but the hours

Juggling childcare and a career as a policewoman was going to prove a bit tricky

and style of policing are more suitable to parenthood. Fortunately, the police career is the type that can be resurrected, so in three or four years' time I may then choose to step back into my previous role.

I have found childcare a difficult issue too, but this is mainly because I do not work a straightforward nine-to-five day from Monday to Friday, and all childminders and nurseries seem to be geared towards this style of parent. After many phone calls and nursery visits, we have finally found a nursery that will take Max for the hours we are looking for, which has pretty much made up our minds for us. I was absolutely flabbergasted with the nursery set-up. Most of them had year-long waiting lists, which meant that some parents were putting their children's names down when they were just five or six weeks pregnant! We were lucky enough to get Max into one due to a cancellation, otherwise he might have been having his first birthday before being accepted.

When Max was born, Bruce announced to me that we would not be having any more children as he could not possibly imagine going through the experience again! I kept quiet, thinking to myself, 'It wasn't *that* bad – I'd give it another go.' Within two months, Bruce had started referring to Max as his 'first born', and again I kept quiet, secretly hoping that he was coming round to my way of thinking about siblings for Max. Now I am pleased to say that Bruce has been talking about names for a brother for Max. I say brother, because Bruce is convinced our next child will be another boy. I think he is so besotted with Max that he is not quite sure how he would handle a girl. I really don't mind, but I can say that I think now I would be happy to stop at two, whatever the sex.

Sarah

* * *

Where do I go from here? A very good question. Do Jack and I go to Spain to live with Tim, who will be working out there for at least twelve to eighteen months, or do I take the modern, working-mother approach and stay in England and return to work? When I left on maternity leave five months ago, I wanted to keep all options open so that I could decide what I wanted to do once my baby was born. I still wish I could lead both lives – a full-time mother and also be able to enjoy the pressures and social interaction of my job. It's only when you reach this point in your life that you become acutely aware of how a woman's incredibly strong maternal instincts, which I wasn't even sure I possessed, conflict with the equally natural desire to feel mentally challenged.

A friend of mine highlighted something interesting when I

was discussing my dilemma with her. She said, 'Of course, there is always that "Identity" issue, isn't there? At work you are Sarah Groves in your own right, and not simply Jack's mother or Tim's wife.' How true, especially when I'm contemplating giving up work and joining my husband in a foreign country where I don't even speak the lingo. Am I prepared to be subjugated to domestic bliss in a place where I have no friends, no social interaction with work colleagues and no daily intellectual stimulation other than baby talk? I could of course take Spanish lessons, but with no one other than the plants and Jack to practise on during the day, my progress may be rather restricted.

But I can see the positives too. The prospect of spending my time on the beach in front of the flat Tim has in Spain and indulging in the hobbies I enjoy most does seem mildly appealing. Shopping, interior decoration, reading and surfing the Internet all day, poor anorak that I am, does sound good, and, of course, I will be getting real quality time bringing up Jack, seeing his every development personally, and not relying on a childminder to report his progress to me each evening when I pick him up after work. I can hear some of you saying, 'Good grief, what an ideal situation! If only my husband would get a job that would allow me to give up work and stay at home soaking up the Spanish sun and bringing up my children,' but I guess the grass is always greener, isn't it?

In short, I think I am now prepared to play at being wife and mother for twelve to eighteen months, but I know that I will still crave the challenge of a job and that identity. I am beginning to think about possibly doing something more artistic at home. Maybe it's time I just faced the fact that my corporate days are over – at least for the foreseeable future, anyway. What I need to do next is find a niche in the Spanish market – something I can fill with British know-how, or the other way round! I can positively say that I have loved these first few months of Jack's life, introducing him to the world and caring for his every need. I am not like one of my friends, who loves children so much that she is expecting her second one when her first will only be eighteen months old, but I have to say that I certainly look forward to having more. Tim and I have discussed numbers, and he has always been keen on the idea of five children. I would personally prefer an even number and I don't think I'd be content with just two. So perhaps this next generation of Groves will be quite numerous! A friend who guessed that I was pregnant with Jack even before I suspected it myself has suggested that I profit from my time in Spain, and make more babies. Thanks for the advice, Heather, but I think I'll have a cooling-off period first! Then again, I do hold the opinion that if you bang them out quickly, you have them all close enough in age to be good friends, and you get your own life back in shape sooner. So many decisions, we shall just have to wait and see.

Annette

***

Before Emily was born, if I had been asked what my postnatal plans were, my response would have rolled off the tongue quickly and confidently. I would be returning to work when Emily was fourteen weeks old on a full-time basis, with Emily going straight into nursery. I would continue with my current career path, and life would not be radically different!

But I had really underestimated my maternal feelings, and after fourteen weeks at home I wanted to stay at home with Emily. We were having a great time, and I did not want things to change – she was the perfect child, with a happy gentle nature and good sleeping habits. Gavin, however, had different ideas, partly because he knows me inside-out and knew that in the longer term I would need intellectual stimulation, and partly for the monthly pay packet we were so used to receiving. Despite my pleas and buckets full of tears, I was told that I *was* going back to work. We would all see how we got on for the first three months and then review the situation. At the time, I remember thinking he was a hard and heartless git, but looking back he was right. I had to try returning to work while the opportunity was still there. If I had not gone back after fourteen weeks, then my job would not have been held open, and the thought of having to undertake interviews at a later date terrified me. They say that your brain shrinks during pregnancy, and I have no idea when it recovers or even if it ever does – I certainly wouldn't relish the prospect of selling myself in an interview now. It was hard enough before with my previous professional confidence. I think I would have settled for shelf-stacking in the local supermarket if I had not gone back to work when I did, which, appealing as it might be, would have been a bit of a waste of all those years studying accounting!

The first drama before returning to work was the settling-in period at nursery. Emily was being difficult about taking a bottle and I was not looking forward to the painful hurdle of weaning her off the breast. When I had first looked around the nursery and booked a place, I was only four months pregnant and I thought it looked efficient. I also knew that it had a good reputation due to the long waiting lists. But when I looked around the nursery as a mother, I just kept thinking how young the staff were, and wondering whether they were old enough to know how to look after a baby, but I had to put these silly thoughts to the back of my mind and proceed with the induction.

The dramatic emotional battle of weaning Emily off the breast, coupled with the trauma of handing over my precious child to these total strangers really took its toll on me. I hated the induction period and dreaded D-Day. When my first day at work arrived, it really was quite peculiar. After all the build-up of settling Emily into nursery and saying goodbye to my sociable afternoons with the other girlies, there was an eerie feeling of complete normality about the whole process! It was refreshing to discover once again that I could actually achieve quite a lot in a day rather than simply nappy changing, feeding and entertaining Emily.

Unfortunately, things did not run that smoothly with the

nursery. Don't get me wrong, I did finally develop confidence in the nursery staff and Emily soon fitted into the seemingly standard nursery model of being a happy if grubby baby. After a while, I was even able to enjoy my lunchtime shopping trips

I was tempted to invest in a pair of overalls to get me through the morning

without that deep-pitted pang of guilt hitting me every time I saw another young mum out with her baby. The morning routine took a little fine-tuning: Emily nicely mastered the art of either vomiting down my suit or filling her nappy just as we were due to set off. I was tempted to invest in a pair of overalls to get me through the morning until I dropped Emily off, but I held back from this purchase mainly from fear of forgetting to remove them and turning up at the office looking as if I had come to repair the boiler. This would have really finished off my colleagues' opinion of me completely!

Emily developed bronchitis after just four weeks at nursery

and was not well enough to attend. The infection took for ever for her to fight, and I ended up having to hire a temporary nanny. It broke my heart having to go to work when she was not well, especially leaving her in the hands of a total stranger when she should have had her mother with her. So now, after just a couple of months at work, course after course of antibiotics for Emily and total trauma for me, I have finally handed in my notice and I am going to do part-time work through an agency. This was a tough decision, but Gavin has been really supportive through it. At first I felt as though I had failed as a working mum, and that I could not cope with the dual role. I realize now, though, that I could cope with it, it was just that I did not want to at the expense of not caring for my daughter when she needed me most – after all, you only get this precious time once!

Our future plans are quite clear now. We have sold our house, which we lovingly restored, and we plan to move closer to one of our sets of parents so that they can help us out occasionally. I want to work on my own terms, but not full-time. This may sound unrealistic, but I am determined to find the right balance so that I do not feel that I am missing out on Emily's life.

Would I have another baby? Yes, I definitely would. Like Sarah and Hilary, two seems too few, but four seems quite a large family! I cannot believe how our life has changed and, remarkably, this is for the better. I do not think I have ever been as happy as I have been over the last five months. I was not unhappy before, but life seems so much richer now with Emily around. We don't miss out on many things. Basically, wherever we go Emily comes along too. We probably go out less as a couple than we used to, but it does not appear to bother us. As aged as it sounds, we are now quite happy having an evening in front of the television with a video and a take-away, followed by a reasonable night's sleep!

Four Years On

Hilary and David now have a second daughter, Isabella (Ella), who was born the week of Molly's second birthday. They were delighted with her safe arrival, as they had suffered a miscarriage prior to this pregnancy. Hilary did return to work as planned for two and a half days a week after six months' maternity leave for both children. When Molly was three and a half, though, she reduced to just one working day when the juggle between village school nursery and day nursery became too much for Molly's sensitive nature to cope with. Hilary and David are now apprehensively pleased to say that they are expecting their third child. The timing is well planned to coincide with Molly going full-time to the village school and Ella doing half days at the village playgroup. Hopefully, this will help Hilary as she adapts to dividing herself, as a mum, three ways. Hilary and David are pretty certain that this will be their last child, but then again, never say never!

Sarah and Tim lived in Spain, regularly commuting between their two homes, until Jack was two and a half years old. Sadly, during this time they lost two babies, both in the second trimester of pregnancy. A medical reason for this was never identified but Sarah and Tim decided to avoid the stress of international commuting before trying again. Tim changed to a UK-based company, and once they had settled back into their home in England Sarah fell pregnant again. Thankfully, she gave birth to a beautiful healthy daughter, Eloise, shortly after Jack's third birthday. Due to her initial international lifestyle, Sarah obviously did not return to work. She currently remains content with her role as a full-time mum, and has no immediate plans to return to work. The jury is out as to whether Sarah and Tim will have any further children. However, they feel that the time for decisions is fast approaching, as Jack has just started full-time education at a local private school. There is something so grown up about Jack and his big buddy Max striding into school together in their smart school blazers. It is enough to begin to numb the pain of the babies lost and start debating the option of a third child in the Groves household.

Lyndsey and Tim have moved nearer to their work places, but Lyndsey still regularly meets the others with Bethan on her day off. She is working a four-day week and Bethan continues to attend day nursery, which she loves. Up until Bethan was nearly two, Lyndsey and Tim were adamant that Bethan would remain an only child. They then changed their minds, though, and started trying for a second. Two long years and two emotionally draining early miscarriages later, they are thrilled to announce that, God willing, they too are expecting their second child. The delayed timing of this has actually proved to be quite fortuitous, as Lyndsey's maternity leave should coincide with Bethan commencing at the local school. This will give Lyndsey the chance to see her settled in for her first term and find a local childminder to provide after-school care, for when she returns to work again.

Andrea and Bruce now have a second son, Sam, who arrived safely after an extremely traumatic pregnancy. Andrea endured persistent bleeding, spina-bifida and cystic-fibrosis scares and fortnightly scans, only to have her waters break at thirty-four weeks, triggered by an exciting visit to watch Arsenal! She then gave birth at thirty-five weeks and, despite initial concerns, Sam is now fighting fit and proving to be far easier on the outside! Sam is a similar age to Ella, and their friendship is proving to be equally as strong as that of their older siblings. Molly and Max have always been very close, and are constantly reminding us that they will get married one day. It is just a shame that Hilary and Andrea didn't give a little more consideration to naming their second children. The combination of 'Sam and Ella' not only sounds like a nightmare dose of food poisoning, but is generally a nightmare dose of mischief!

Andrea also returned to work after six-month maternity leaves for both of her children, and now continues to work a three-day week as a community police officer. Andrea would love to have more children, but now fully accepts that Sam will be her last on the grounds that Bruce, a loving dad to two children, has made it perfectly clear that a third child would also mean a divorce! As Sam now approaches playgroup age, and Max is at full-time school with Jack, Andrea is considering her career options again and is currently debating whether to sit her Sergeants exam.

Annette and Gavin had their second daughter, Megan, when Emily was just sixteen months old. This was a bit of a shock, but a pleasant one! They did move nearer to Gavin's parents and initially lived with them while they restored their new home. Unfortunately, just after they moved into their new home, when Megan was only a few months old, Annette was diagnosed with bowel cancer and started undergoing regular chemotherapy sessions. Shortly after Megan's first birthday, Annette was told that the cancer had spread to her liver and that there was no cure. Annette remained so strong and was determined to be a ground-breaking first to beat this cruel disease. She underwent every possible course of treatment, both homeopathic and medical, in order to prolong her life for as long as possible. Tragically, despite all Annette's positive thinking and ferocious fighting, she lost her battle with cancer just six months later, on 13 April 2000. At the tender age of thirty-one, she left behind her husband Gavin and her two beautiful little girls, Emily and Megan, who were then both under the age of three.

Despite the geographical distance, the rest of the fat ladies have pledged to make sure that they stay emotionally close to Emily and Megan. A few days before Annette died, we sat with her and helped her to write letters to her daughters, which she wanted read to them at various key stages in their lives. Annette then entrusted the responsibility for this task to Andrea. Since Annette's death, Andrea has made sure that as many as possible of the fat ladies and their children spend at least four weekends a year with Annette's children. They are growing up so fast, and with each visit Emily is more noticeably developing into a mirror image of her mother, both in personality and looks. Megan is a lovely, lively bundle of fun, but sadly she was so young when her mum died that she doesn't have the same understanding of who we are and why we visit.

Despite this, the times when we are all together with Emily and Megan are moments that we always treasure, because this is the closest we come to our club being complete. The Fat Ladies Club could never actually feel complete again, but we are all so proud to have shared this writing experience with Annette, and therefore be able to ensure that she lives on in this book as the fun, kind and totally selfless person she was.

Annette was a fantastic mum and a very dear and loyal friend. She will always be with us, the four remaining members of the Fat Ladies Club.

One-sixth of all authors' profits from the sale of this book are donated to Colon Cancer Concern (reg. charity no. 1071038) in memory of our fabulous friend,

Annette Louise Jones
2 Dec 1968–13 April 2000.